Ireland

100 Legendary Places

ROUGH GUIDES

Ireland

100 Legendary Places

Ireland
100 Legendary Places

Introduction

Ireland's legends are not confined to old stories. They are held in stone forts and monastic valleys, in wind-scoured islands, music-filled pubs, famine roads, Georgian squares, castle ruins and cliff paths where the Atlantic seems to have the final word. An island split politically in two, its history has often been turbulent, but its beauty and warm welcome remain constant, whether you travel north or south.

This book gathers 100 legendary places across Ireland, from the famous to the quietly extraordinary. Some are fixed firmly in the national imagination, including Newgrange, the Rock of Cashel, the Giant's Causeway, Glendalough, Skellig Michael and the Cliffs of Moher. Others work more subtly, through character and atmosphere: a remote island community, a garden hidden down country roads, a village with music at its heart, a hill associated with kingship, or a city wall that holds centuries of conflict and endurance in its stones.

Ireland is a place in which to slow down and take it all in. These 100 places form a journey through cities, islands, mountains, beaches, sacred sites, cultural landmarks and local curiosities – the celebrated, the strange, the beautiful, the storied, and the deeply local.

My Goodness-
a 200th birthday label!
Lovely day for a GUINNESS
PLEASE DON'T CLIMB ON THE RAILINGS

GUINNESS

Dublin

The Republic's capital is compact, sociable and endlessly absorbing. This is a city of Georgian squares, literary ghosts, great museums – and famously, pubs with great craic. The Liffey splits northside from southside, each offering its own sort of swagger, while beaches, headlands and Phoenix Park offer easy escape not far away. Historic prisons, galleries, stadiums and breweries sit close together, giving Dublin a rare mix of intimacy, energy and cultural weight.

ROAR
OF
GUINNESS
DUBLIN
GUINNESS
DUBLIN
758373
GUINNESS
DUBLIN
273589
RAW
SMELLS
GUINNESS
DUBLIN
625368
GUINNESS
DUBLIN
773582
GUINNESS
DUBLIN
625353
ROAR
OF
RAW
GUINNESS
DUBLIN

Guinness Storehouse

It goes without saying that no visit to Dublin, or indeed Ireland, is complete without a pint or two of the black stuff. But better than that, go and see how it is produced. The Guinness Storehouse is a seven-storey building built around a soaring glass atrium in the shape of a pint of beer – which would contain 14.3 million pints if full. It's located on the main road out of the city, in between the Irish Museum of Modern Art and St Patrick's Cathedral. The building pays homage to the history of the perennially popular stout, from its founding in 1759 when Arthur Guinness began brewing on the site, through to the brewing process itself and an exhibition on the company's legendary marketing campaigns – the Guinness White Horses advert, anyone? Naturally, there are plenty of opportunities to sup a pint during your visit, in particular up on the rooftop Gravity Bar, where a free pint is included as part of the admission. Hell, why stop there? Kick back with another whilst observing the comings and goings on the streets below or stay for lunch. And whilst you don't necessarily have to be a fan of the tipple to make this a worthwhile trip, it certainly helps.

(L) The brewing process explained in the on-site exhibition

James Joyce Pilgrimage

It's not too far-fetched to suggest that it was *Ulysses* – the modernist masterpiece by the Irish author James Joyce and a book referred to by TS Eliot as "one to which we are all indebted, and from which none of us can escape" – that really put Dublin on the international map. And it is why so many Joyce aficionados make the pilgrimage to the birthplace of the literary titan. Start at the statue of the great man on North Earl Street before taking in the James Joyce Centre and then head across the river towards St Stephen's Green and the Museum of Literature Ireland; both the centre and museum are full to bursting with Joycean treasures. Hunt down, too, the fourteen brass plaques laid in pavements around the city which mark out the walk taken by the novel's chief protagonist Leopold Bloom during the course of the day. The big day to be here is Bloomsday on 16 June – the date on which the novel's events took place in 1904 – when the city is awash with Joycean jollity, courtesy of readings, talks, re-enactments, singing, food, fancy dress (boater hats at the ready), and tonnes more literary lunacy.

(L) The man himself; (T) Man in Bloomsday costume at the James Joyce Centre; (B) Bloomsday performance at Davy Byrnes pub

Kilmainham Gaol

(T) The historic jail

One of the largest unoccupied jails in Europe, Kilmainham Gaol's history is writ large. Opened in 1796, it became the place of incarceration for captured revolutionaries, including rebel leaders of the failed 1916 uprising; fourteen of them were also executed here. Left to rot following its closure in 1924, the gaol was given a new lease of life in the 1960s before being transformed into the visitor attraction it is today. Tours of the jail reveal the prisoners' bleak living conditions, its single cells ensuring that they were forced into solitary contemplation, and since the building was constructed on top of limestone, their health was badly affected by damp and severe cold in winter. Exhibition galleries offer an account of the struggle for independence, courtesy of numerous mementos and cinematic footage. Indeed, Kilmainham has featured prominently as a film location – *Michael Collins* and *In the Name of the Father* among them – while even dear old Paddington Bear did a stint serving porridge here in *Paddington 2*.

38

National Gallery *of* Ireland

Ireland's foremost gallery is a sprawling institution housing the best of the nation's art, including the National Portrait Collection, as well as a dazzling spread of European masterpieces and rotating contemporary exhibitions. Don't forget to pick up a map before you dive in, with four massive wings to explore. Highlights include Caravaggio's *The Taking of Christ*, a number of works from Rembrandt, Monet and their contemporaries, fine paintings by Spanish artists from Goya to Picasso, and much more besides. In-depth guided tours are an ideal way to explore this treasure trove. Time it right and you'll be able to see *Hellelil and Hildebrand*, the *Meeting on the Turret Stairs* by Frederic William Burton, unveiled only for an hour on Thursday and Sunday afternoons to protect its delicate watercolours from light exposure. Sculpture, photography and furniture all feature alongside paintings, drawings and prints in this expansive gallery.

(O) Inside the gallery; (L) The imposing exterior; (T) Appreciating fine art

Howth Cliff Walk

Clinging to the slopes of a rocky peninsula and overlooking an animated fishing harbour, the village of Howth (rhymes with 'both'), at the end of the DART line has a wonderful Cliff Walk. The route takes in great views south over the city to the Wicklow Mountains and north to the Boyne Valley. The footpath runs for some 8km clockwise from the village round to the west-facing side of the peninsula, followed by a 3km walk by the sea along Strand Road and Greenfield Road to Sutton DART station – allow at least three hours. You first head east out of Howth village along Balscadden Road to the Nose of Howth, before the path turns south, crossing the slopes above the cliffs, which are covered in colourful gorse and bell heather in season; the area known as the Summit, just inland of the path, has a pub and a café. The southeast point is marked by the Baily Lighthouse. The path along the south-facing coast of the peninsula is the most spectacular part of the walk, offering sublime views of cliffs, secluded beaches and rocky islands.

(L) Howth Head; (T, B) Howth hiking tour

Wicklow, Kildare & Meath

Wrapping around Dublin, the counties of Wicklow, Kildare and Meath move from mountain solitude to horse country and ancient royal ground. Wicklow is home to granite hills, wooded estates and the ruins of Glendalough. Kildare softens into grassland, studs and grand houses. Meath carries older authority, with passage tombs, sacred hills and Norman castles rising from lush farmland, making this region feel both close to the Irish capital, and far deeper in time.

Avondale Forest Park

Avondale is a multi-sensory joy: listen to the sweetest birdsong and the gentle rustle of leaves; feel the breeze dance across your shoulders; and experience a rush of adrenaline as the forest floor disappears beneath your feet. Take delight in interactive, educational displays and dart across lofty bridges marked by bursts of brightly painted flowers. As you gently ascend into the canopies of the trees, the beauty of nature is literally all around you. Trace the looping pathway of the Treetop Walk before climbing the spiralling Viewing Tower to its dizzying summit: a 124ft-high lookout platform. Once there, stop to soak in the exceptional viewpoints north, south, east and west, before the final adrenalin kick – a super slide that will rocket you back down to earth, and fast. Back on firm ground, giddy from the thrill, regain your composure with a browse in the giftshop or wander over to the café with its playground and pretty courtyard garden. For those with a zest for more, hours of walking is possible on the five hundred-acre grounds of the Forest Park, while history buffs might enjoy a visit to Avondale House. Those keen to experience it all over again needn't fear, Avondale's treetop magic will call you back again.

(L) Aerial view of Avondale House and the Treetop Walk

Mount Usher

Designed by Dubliner Edward Walpole in 1868, in the Robinsonian style made famous by the eponymous gardener, Mount Usher Gardens shelter a plethora of rare trees, shrubs and flowers, including dazzling rhododendrons, azaleas and maples, and the finest eucalyptus specimens in Europe. It's all growing in an informal style in its woodlands and meadows in Ashford, County Wicklow, just 35 minutes outside of Dublin city centre and serviced by bus number 133. Running through the gardens is the River Vartry, broken up here by a remarkable series of nineteenth-century weirs, watercourses and suspension bridges. The Avoca café on site will ensure you remain well fed and refreshed while the Courtyard Shops are a tempting diversion. Come on a sunny day and delight in one of the country's finest gardens.

(O) The gardens; (L) Suspension bridges cross the river throughout the gardens; (T) Riverside pathways; (B) A river runs through it...

Glendalough

A deep glaciated valley in the heart of the Wicklow Mountains, Glendalough (valley of the two lakes) provides a delightfully atmospheric location for some of the best-preserved monastic sites in Ireland and some lovely, marked walking trails. Despite the coach hordes, enough of the valley's tranquillity remains for you to understand what drew monks and pilgrims here. The main monastic site and visitor facilities are on the eastern side of the Lower Lake, while further west up the valley is the more impressive Upper Lake, with its wooded cliffs and dramatic waterfall. It's enjoyable to walk from the Deer Stone along the Green Road (part of the Wicklow Way), a scenic track that skirts the south side of the Lower Lake. This will bring you to the tiny, ruined, late tenth century-Romanesque Reefert Church, whose cemetery is said to contain the graves of local chieftains. From here a path runs up to St Kevin's Cell, the remains of a beehive hut on a promontory overlooking the lake. One of Glendalough's most famous monuments, the 30m-high Round Tower, is nestled in a valley close to the Lower Lake.

(L) Glendalough Graveyard; (T) The Upper Lake and loop walking trail; (B) St Kevin's Church

Huntingbrook

(T) A dazzling summer display

Jimi Blake, the owner and creator of Huntingbrook Gardens, began the transformation of twenty acres of a County Wicklow woodland valley in 2001, developing it into a highly regarded and internationally renowned garden full of unusual plant combinations, divided into five areas, each with their own style. Ashley's Garden showcases Jimi's famous exotic and vibrant planting, with many species having been brought back from China. Fred's Garden shows off contrasting textures, while the Sand Garden features succulents and cacti. The Woodland Garden is sheltered by deciduous and coniferous trees, and boasts huge collections of snowdrops and epimediums. Finally, The Valley is both stunning and peaceful, with views over the Wicklow Mountains and glimpses of a ring fort and standing stones. Planting includes collections of rhododendrons, acers and magnolias. Jimi's style is unconventional and the gardens are ever-changing, sometimes with plants no one would expect to survive in Ireland.

National Stud

It's no secret that the Irish profess a deep-rooted attachment to all things equine, something that's very much in evidence at the Irish National Stud on the Curragh in Kildare, an hour or so southwest of Dublin. The stud was established in 1900 by Colonel William Hall Walker, of Scotch whisky fame, whose methods were as eccentric as they were successful: each newborn foal's horoscope was read, and those on whom the stars didn't shine were sold, regardless of their lineage or physical characteristics. Presented to the British government in 1915 – henceforth known as the British National Stud – it was finally transferred to the Irish government in 1944. There's a day's worth of entertainment here, from tours of the stud and a visit to the Irish Racehorse Experience – where you get the opportunity to own, train and race your own thoroughbred, as well as have a go at some commentary, to a stroll around the fabled Japanese Gardens. But the stars, of course, are the horses themselves. The Living Legends field is home to many retired prize horses; indeed, many a great racehorse has been raised here.

(L) Million-euro horses at the Irish National Stud; (T, B) The Irish Racehorse Experience

Castletown House

Castletown House is a beautiful Palladian mansion in County Kildare, considered to be the finest example of the style in Ireland. Extensive restoration had to be carried out on the building after it was left vacant and vandalised in the 1960s, and it became the flagship project of the Irish Georgian Society. Most of its contents having been sold off, also in the '60s, extraordinary efforts have been made in subsequent years to buy back furniture, paintings and other decorative items which are now on display. However, the curiosity of the Wonderful Barn may be considered by some to be the main attraction. Certainly not what you expect to find when looking for a 'barn', this corkscrew-shaped building baffles visitors. The generally accepted view is that was built as a store for grain, and to provide employment following the famine of the 1740s. Unfortunately, it is not possible to enter the building, but the view of it alone is worth the trip.

(O) Castletown House; (L) The Wonderful Barn;
(T) The opulent drawing room

Newgrange

Newgrange is unquestionably the most striking of the Brú na Bóinne mounds, not least because its facade of white quartz stones and round granite boulders has been reassembled. The quartz originally came from Wicklow, the granite from the Mourne and Carlingford areas, exemplifying the mind-boggling levels of resources and organisation lavished on this project, by these farmers who used nothing but simple tools of wood and stone. It has been estimated that the tumulus, which is over 75m in diameter, weighs 200,000 tons in total and would have taken around forty years to build. It was the final resting place of a high-status family within the Neolithic community – the cremated remains and grave goods of at least five people were recovered from the burial chamber during excavation – but seems also to have had a wider purpose as a ritual site or gathering place. The entrance stone is one of the finest examples of the art of the tomb-builders, who carved spectacular but enigmatic spirals, chevrons, lozenges and other geometric designs onto many of the large stones around the mound and up the 19m passage. The tomb's pivotal feature, however, is a roof-box above the entrance whose slit was perfectly positioned to receive the first rays of the rising sun on the day of the winter solstice (21 December); the light first peeps into the cruciform burial chamber itself before spreading its rays along the length of the passage.

(L) Winter solstice sunrise

Hill of Tara

Perhaps more than anywhere else in Ireland, the Hill of Tara carries the weight of both history and myth. Best known as the ritual seat of the High Kings, this long, grass-covered rise in County Meath had already been a major ceremonial site for millennia before kingship gathered around it. Its power is not in spectacle, but in atmosphere: circular mounds, ditches, barrows and earthworks lie low in the turf, while the surrounding countryside opens out in every direction. Irish sagas place gods, queens and semi-divine rulers here, and later history has only deepened its pull, from dynastic struggles to Daniel O'Connell's huge Repeal meeting in 1843. Tara is best approached in an unhurried way. The remains need a little imagination, but the setting itself does much of the work, especially when the wind moves across the hill and the old kingdom suddenly feels closer than the passing of time might suggest.

(L) The earthworks; (T) Frosty morning at the Hill of Tara; (B) Sunset at the Summer Solstice

Trim Castle

War raged in Ireland for many centuries of its long and distinguished history, reflected in the roughly 30,000 castles and fortifications that stud the land. These are not the show castles of royals and gentry as found in England and the rest of Europe, but fortified seats and outposts built by chieftains or invaders. County Meath's Trim Castle is the mightiest fortress in Ireland, standing or otherwise, stretching over 30sq km. The largest Anglo-Norman castle ruin in Europe, it took thirty years to construct under Hugh de Lacy and his inheritors in the twelfth and thirteenth centuries. From an impregnable fortress against the Celts it grew in the following centuries, becoming a mint for currency in the fifteenth century and meeting point for parliament before eventually falling to Cromwell's occupation in 1649. Walking through its gates and along its ramparts, you might recognise its modern use as a filming location during the siege of King John's castle in *Braveheart* starring Mel Gibson. It's free to enter the grounds.

(O) The castle illuminated after dark; (L) Internal stairway; (T) Kayaking on the Boyne beside the castle; (B) The Keep

Louth, Monaghan & Cavan

The counties of Louth, Monaghan and Cavan sit along the borderlands, where big houses, planned towns and older religious sites reveal layers of Plantation, myth and local memory. Louth is small but historically rich, with the Boyne valley and the Cooley mountains giving it scale. Monaghan's drumlins and literary associations lend a quieter charm, while Cavan is shaped by lakes, waterways and rugged uplands, best explored slowly, map in hand.

Cooley Peninsula

Separated from the north of Ireland only by Carlingford Lough, the largely off-the-radar Cooley Peninsula is a rounded 15km plug of Irish turf and granite, a beautiful and dramatic landscape bearing green-shouldered hills crested with crags and gently sloping valleys. Cooley's main settlement is colourful Carlingford, erstwhile Viking settlement but now all fifteenth-century walls and fortified townhouses, narrow cobbled streets and white-stone cottages – but above all, it seems, an endless succession of quintessential Irish boozers. The peninsula is also home to what is arguably the definitive Irish legend, that of the Táin Bó Cuailnge (Cattle Raid of Cooley), an epic pagan odyssey of greed and self-sacrifice set around 500BC. The saga has lent its name to the 40km-long Táin Way, a circular route around Slieve Foye (587m). More doable is the Greenway, which skims the lough all the way to Omeath, 7km away – terrific on foot or by bike.

(O) Dramatic views of the peninsula; (L) Hiking the Cooley Peninsula; (R) Carlingford town

THE Jumping Church

(T) The remains of the jumping wall

Ireland is hardly devoid of outlandish tourist attractions, and folklore comes as standard wherever you go, but few places elicit as much intrigue as the Jumping Church in Kildemock, just south of the town of Ardlee in central County Louth. The mystery swirling around Millockstown Church (as it's formally known) revolves around how the western wall mysteriously 'jumped' to land some 3ft within the building's own foundations – hence the nickname 'Jumping Wall'. All manner of dubious theories have been posited, among them that the wall leapt inwards to exclude an unworthy corpse from the holy ground of the church interior, while another supposes that a violent storm caused the west gable of the building to move eastwards, leaving it standing in its improbable new position within the ediface. Spooky goings-on aside, this is a wonderfully tranquil spot, the church positioned atop a hill with the Carlingford and Mourne mountains providing a suitably ethereal backdrop.

Castle Leslie Estate

Fancy a spot of fishing or falconry, some horse riding, a carriage ride or perhaps a seaweed peat bath followed by a scrumptious meal and a positively perfect night's kip? Then Castle Leslie Estate, set on a thousand acres of County Monaghan countryside in the neat little village of Glaslough, ticks all those boxes. An almost unaltered Victorian playground built in 1871 for Sir John Leslie, 1st baronet, Castle Leslie Estate – which is still home to the founding family – is pure Gothic fantasy, fashioned in Scottish baronial style, all spiky turrets, marbled fireplaces and an extravagant library that, according to the author Jonathan Swift (one of the castle's many esteemed guests), possessed "rows of books upon its shelves, written by Leslies all about themselves". Dining-wise, take your pick from the award-winning Snaffles Restaurant or enjoy a more relaxed style 'pub grub' in Conor's Bar, both at The Lodge. They even serve a fabulous afternoon tea. Whatever your bed or table of choice, one thing is guaranteed: you'll have little urge to leave whatsoever.

(L) Ready for flight; (T) Aerial view of the estate; (B) One of the sumptuous bedrooms

THE Kavanagh Trail

There is no doubt that Patrick Kavanagh ranks alongside those other titans of Irish literature – namely Yeats and Heaney – yet acclaim for the poet remains largely confined to his homeland. Born in 1904 in Inniskeen, an unassuming rural backwater some 12km west of Dundalk – Kavanagh lived on a small farm here for the first 35 years of his life, before moving to Dublin. At the heart of the village stands St Mary's Church, whose annexe houses the brilliantly transformed Patrick Kavanagh Centre, packed full of Kavanagh-related memorabilia, including photographs, manuscripts and his death mask, memory boxes containing personal effects, and touch screens, as well as a specially commissioned series of twelve paintings based upon his epic and extraordinarily emotive poem *The Great Hunger*. In late September the village plays host to a festival celebrating their much-loved local poet. True devotees of the man can take a gander along the 6km-long Kavanagh Trail, a dedicated dual-use path that takes in all the prominent Kavanagh landmarks, like his former homestead in Mucker, Billy Brennan's barn – the vernacular farm buildings immortalised in Inniskeen Road: July Evening – and Shancoduff, 'the triangular field under the Big Forth'. His grave, along with that of his wife, can be found in the church cemetery.

(L) St Mary's Church and its graveyard

Cavan Burren Park

A vast, wind-whipped limestone plateau, the Cavan Burren Park is loaded with one of Ireland's greatest troves of prehistoric treasures – megalithic tombs, cist graves and ancient stone huts – yet it's one of the least known parts of the country. Tucked away well off the tourist trail on the border between north and south, the Cavan Burren Park is a wild, desolately beautiful spot. One monument, the Giant's Grave, is nearly 8m-long and composed of one-tonne slabs arranged to align with the setting sun. Another, the Calf House, is a tomb the size of a garden shed, complete with a great hulk of stone slumped at 45 degrees; the original tomb dates back to around 4000BC but at some point a local farmer saw fit to build a wall into it, converting it into a calf shelter. A basic but informative open-air visitor centre helps make sense of this otherworldly landscape, and is also the starting point for a series of short, looped walks through the park, ranging in length from 1.3km to 3km, the shortest of which is wheelchair accessible.

(O) The Calf House; (L) Beautiful walking trails; (T) Trail through the park; (B) Wildflowers bordering one of the walking trails

Westmeath, Longford, Offaly & Laois

Too often crossed in a hurry, the Midlands reward anyone who stops. Westmeath's lakes, Longford's quiet grasslands, Offaly's bogs and Laois's rolling country hold some of Ireland's most atmospheric surprises: ancient trackways, monastic ruins, scientific estates, old pubs and commanding hilltop remains. The Shannon gives the region a slow, reflective mood, while its towns and villages preserve a rural rhythm that feels natural and unforced, rather than staged for curious visitors.

Hill of Uisneach

Uisneach (roughly pronounced 'ish-knack') is the sacred and mythological centre of Ireland; site of Bealtaine fires and Druidical ceremonies. Situated in Rathnew, County Westmeath, at 596ft above sea level, there are views of the central plain of Ireland with twenty counties visible. Surviving monuments and relics range in date from Neolithic, early Bronze Age and the Medieval period, including a megalithic tomb, burial mounds, enclosures, standing stones, holy wells and a ceremonial road. Uisneach is the mythological resting place of Ériu, goddess of Ireland who gave her name to the country, and it was the original seat of the High Kings of Ireland before this passed to Tara in neighbouring County Meath. It remained the meeting point for the ancient provinces where deals were struck. It was linked to Tara by a ceremonial road, a section of which remains today. Today the site is still used to celebrate the coming of summer with the Bealtaine festival, when a fire is lit on the hill and there is music, art installations, talks and games. Guided tours of the site provide interpretation of Uisneach's features and history.

(L) Hill of Uisneach; (T) Bealtaine festivities; (B) Dressing up in medieval costume

Kilbeggan Distillery

Kilbeggan Distillery is the oldest operational distillery in Ireland and, apart from an interlude in the twentieth century, has been turning out some of the nation's finest whiskey for over two hundred years. While lesser known, it's a must-see for whiskey lovers. It may not surprise you that the booze business contains its fair share of controversy and criminality, of which Kilbeggan claims a respectable slice – from wanted lawbreakers under alias looking to flip its whiskey on English black markets, to the execution of the original founder's son for his part in the failed revolt of 1798. Doggedly beating back financial woes from every angle over its illustrious lifespan, today you'll find Kilbeggan to be a welcoming and fully functioning distillery. Deep biscuity aromas will greet your arrival along with the rushing waters of the River Brosna, pouring through the distillery's nineteenth-century water wheel still used to power machinery inside. A 'Distillery Experience' tour starts with a whiskey cocktail taster and ends with a four-glass masterclass in whiskey sampling.

(O) The old distillery building; (L) The distillery vats from the outside; (T) The nineteenth-century water wheel; (B) The whiskey barrels

Seans Bar
Irelands Oldest Pub
As Listed In
GUINNESS Book Of
World Records
Seans
Bar

Sean's Bar

Dating from 900AD, Sean's Bar is the oldest in Ireland and is located only a few steps from Athlone's Norman castle. Renovations during the 1970s revealed that the walls were constructed from wattle and wicker, a section of which can be seen in the bar behind a glass panel, the remainder being housed for preservation in Ireland's National Museum. With such a pedigree, the atmosphere does not disappoint, while the open fire and sawdust floor will mean you will gladly settle into this cosy bar for the evening. Outside at the rear of the bar a sheltered beer garden has been created which overlooks the River Shannon. Explore the neighbouring streets which are full of bars, restaurants and independent shops. Maybe work up a thirst by visiting Athlone Castle, where you can learn about the history of this important fortification on the River Shannon through interactive displays and demonstrations. Or take a walk along the banks of the Shannon and watch the boats come and go from the Marina.

(L) Enjoy the terrace on a sunny day

Corlea Trackway

In the boglands of south County Longford, a togher or bog road was discovered in the 1980s in an area where peat was industrially harvested. This pathway, constructed from heavy planks of oak, was dated using dendrochronological (tree-ring dating) testing to 148BC – contemporaneous with the Siege of Carthage by the Romans. The Corlea Trackway is the largest bog road to have been discovered in Europe. At the visitor centre in Corlea, you can view an 18m-stretch of the trackway in a hall specially designed to preserve it, as well as murals and displays showing people and objects of the era. It is thought that the trackway may have been part of a ceremonial highway connecting the Hill of Uisneach with Rathcroghan. The terrain would have been dangerous and impassable for much of the year, being mainly bog, quicksand and ponds. The trackway remained in use for only a few years before sinking under its own weight and was thus preserved by the bog. During your visit, you can also take a walk across a preserved bog nearby.

(L) Original track; (T) Walking over the bog; (B) The visitor centre

Granard Motte & Bailey

In the north-east of County Longford you will find the highest motte in Ireland at 534ft above sea level, built circa 1199 by Norman knight Richard de Tuite after he was granted lands by Henry II. De Tuite was later made Lord Chief Justice of Ireland. The fortification was erected on and within a pre-existing hillfort as part of an initiative to extend Norman control over Ireland. Originally a timber tower surrounded by a palisade and ditch, Granard Motte and Bailey would have enclosed animals and soldiers. Today of course the timber structures are gone, leaving behind a great flat-topped earthen mound. The summit gives views of five lakes and nine counties. Myths have persisted regarding the hollow within the mound, which some believe contains a castle or gold. Nearby is the Knights and Conquests heritage centre, where you can dress in Norman clothes, receive a Norman name and discover and dig for artefacts in the display room.

(O) A statue of St Patrick watches over the site; (L) Shields at the ready; (T) The motte

Birr Castle

Astronomy, engineering, botany, history-all feature at Birr Castle in County Offaly. It is home to the Great Telescope, the largest telescope in the world when it was built in the 1840s, alongside fifty champion trees and reputedly the largest children's tree house in the country. A castle was originally built on the site during the Anglo-Norman period, but the current building dates from the 1800s, although walls from the very first building still survive. The castle has been home to the Parsons family for centuries and is still occupied as a private family home. The grounds alone are worth seeing however; there is an incredible variety of trees and plants. Mapped trails will take you through some of the fifty hectares of grounds with varied landscape including rivers, waterfalls, a lake as well as formal gardens. There are over 5000 plant species as well as the world's tallest box hedge. The ancient oak trees are a must-see. The Science Centre holds a collection of early electrical and engineering equipment, as well as early astronomical and photographic instruments used by the family.

(O) The castle grounds have many walking trails; (T) The Great Telescope; (B) The Science Centre

Clonmacnoise

(T) Views over the graveyard to the Shannon

While Clonmacnoise is a well-known tourist attraction of the Midlands, travelling there by boat offers a truly impressive view of the ruined monastery from the River Shannon as you approach. The monastery at Clonmacnoise was founded in the sixth century by St Ciaran, and drew scholars from all over Europe, becoming an important seat of learning. Unfortunately, it also became very attractive to the Vikings and Normans, whose attacks contributed to its decline, culminating in its final abandonment in the 1500s. The ruins include a cathedral, several churches, two round towers and three high crosses, and all have been sensitively conserved. An interesting feature of the cathedral is a doorway known as the Whispering Arch which, it is said, was used for confession by lepers – they could stand on one side and whisper their sins, and the structure of the doorway would allow the monk standing on the other side to hear without getting too close. Visitors today can try it for themselves.

Lough Boora Discovery Park

Lough Boora Discovery Park is the result of the rehabilitation of the land following decades of peat harvesting for the supply of Ireland's power stations and homes. While the destruction of Ireland's raised peat bogs is certainly nothing to be proud of, the example provided by Lough Boora in Offaly of how the land can be restored with both nature and community in mind is inspiring. This free amenity not only provides walking and cycling trails through a variety of landscapes, but it is also a sanctuary for a variety of flora and fauna. The park boasts an archaeological site dating to the Mesolithic Age providing evidence that the Midlands of Ireland were colonised 3000 years earlier than previously believed. Trails vary in length and can be walked or cycled, including a fairy trail in the woods for the smaller trekkers. Lakes were created here following the end of peat extraction which have now been developed, naturalised and stocked with fish. Many water birds have now made the bog their home and over 130 bird species have been recorded.

(O) Aerial view of the discovery park; (L) Feeding the swans; (T) Sky Train sculpture; (B) Man-made lakes

Rock *of* Dunamase

Rising abruptly from the Laois countryside, the Rock of Dunamase is one of those ruins that seems to have been placed for maximum drama. The shattered walls of the medieval fortress cling to a limestone outcrop, its broken gateways and curtain walls framing big views over the surrounding fields. Its story stretches back through early Christian, Viking and Anglo-Norman Ireland, and the site later became entangled in the dynastic power struggles that shaped Leinster. Yet part of Dunamase's appeal lies in how lightly it is managed. There are no elaborate reconstructions or heavy-handed displays, just rough stone, open sky and the pleasurable scramble of paths through the ruins. From below, it looks imposing and striking. From the top, with the midlands spread around you, the place feels more like a watchpoint than a monument, a place to be alert to movement across the plains.

(L) The ruins from above

Kilkenny, Carlow & Wexford

The southeast feels greener, warmer and more settled than much of Ireland, yet its history is anything but quiet. Kilkenny preserves the country's most atmospheric medieval cityscape, with castle, lanes and cathedral giving it grandeur. Carlow brings gardens, soft hills and unexpected cultural stops. Wexford adds beaches, opera, rebellion, Norman remains and sea light, its coastline moving between family sands, old ports and bleak headlands that face the Channel winds.

Medieval Mile

See the historic sights of Kilkenny city on a walking tour and use the Medieval Mile Museum as your starting point. Formerly St Mary's Church, it is now a museum with 800 years of Kilkenny's history under its roof as well as being a beautiful vantage point to see the city (check out the panoramic window in the Kilkenny Room). From here, take a guided tour or wander out by yourself to see sights such as Kilkenny Castle and Rothe House and Gardens; the latter is well worth a visit during the summer, especially in August for the Kilkenny Arts Festival when there's a whole calendar of concerts alongside pop-up galleries with local art for sale. You'll get local stories and history as well as interesting nuggets of local lore. Afterwards, pop into The Hole in the Wall, the city's oldest and quirkiest bar for a tipple. If still in town and hungry to see more, there is also the Smithwick's Brewery, St Canice's Cathedral and Round Tower (the winding steps to the top are not for the claustrophobic), and across the river, the modern Butler Art Gallery.

(O) Kilkenny Castle; (L) St Canice's Cathedral; (T) Ancient statues on display in the museum; (B) Smithwick's Experience

Inistioge

(T) The stone bridge

Just a 25km drive from Kilkenny City lies the delightful and historic village of Inistioge (pronounced 'innish-teague'). Situated on the River Nore and home to an attractive eighteenth-century stone bridge with no less than ten arches, the historic village has pleasant pubs, an antique shop, art gallery and a café. Unsurprisingly, it has been used on more than one occasion as a set for major film productions due to the many fine period houses (built in the eighteenth and nineteenth centuries) that line the village square. One unusual sight is the location of two churches – St Mary's Church of Ireland, dating from medieval times, and the Roman Catholic church of St Colmcille – standing side by side. Behind the churches are the ruins of a thirteenth-century Augustan Priory. Woodstock House can be found up the steep hill leading from the village. Now sadly just a shell, it has beautiful landscaped gardens and a woodland playground for kids.

Altamont Gardens

Altamont is often referred to as the jewel in Ireland's gardening crown. Situated just outside Tullow, County Carlow, it boasts forty acres of old-world manicured lawns, specimen trees, and informal gardens inspired by the style of Irish horticulturalist William Robinson. Exploring these gardens is easily done on foot, with various walking trails mapping out a route around the lake, Bog Garden, and Ice Age Glen, a riverside woodland walk under impressive oaks. Another trail, the Temple Walk, leads up to a small temple overlooking fields and farmland as far as the eye can see; a place to pause for a moment and watch the barley sway in the breeze. Visit in July and you'll be treated to a beautiful herbaceous border in full bloom. Over 60m-long, it is packed with dahlias, achillea and roses, to name but a few. On site you'll also find a nursery and Sugar & Spice café with indoor and outdoor seating; the latter is dotted with pergolas.

(O) Altamont House; (L) The gardens are full of wonderful specimen plants; (T) The aroma from the rhododendrons is intoxicating

Huntington Castle

There are many delightful things about Huntington Castle in County Carlow, not least the friendly, roaming peacock. Built in the 1600s, the castle is privately owned by the Durdin Robertsons, who live there and open it to the public. Take a guided castle tour to explore the original Tapestry Room and all its fineries, the conservatory with its magnificent grape vine on the ceiling (a gift to Anne Boleyn that came from Hampton Court Palace in London) and take delight in stories of the Temple of the Goddess deep in the castle's dungeon. In the grounds, follow the paths in the formal Italian Parterre, breathe in the scent on the sumptuous rose walk (when in bloom), enjoy the calm Water Gardens and appreciate the changing seasons in the gardens all year round. Youngsters will enjoy the cute Woodland Playground, complete with an obstacle course, play huts, and diggers. The tearooms serve locally baked sweet treats in the seventeenth-century barn next to the castle. During clement weather you can sit out in the pleasant courtyard – just beware that peacock, he has quite a weakness for scones.

(L) The castle is located in the midst of stunnning countryside; (T) Ancient trees line the Yew Walk; (B) The castle up close

Curracloe Beach

Curracloe strand, 11km northeast of Wexford Harbour, is a totally unspoiled, pristine stretch of beach that runs for 10km along some of the country's loveliest coastline. Wedged between untamed dunes and the Atlantic Ocean, it stood in for the Normandy beaches as the site of the D-Day landings when Steven Spielberg filmed *Saving Private Ryan* here in 1998. Extending south is the Raven Nature Reserve, an expanse of dunes and a 600-acre pine forest that stretches down to Raven Point at the mouth of the estuary. The easy 6.5km looped walk through the forest trail is lovely and offers a chance to spot some of the conservation area's protected wildlife such as the red squirrel. Bird enthusiasts will delight – species including the Greenland White-fronted goose, cormorant, red-throated diver, grey plover, common scoter and sanderling can all be spotted. In spring, keep an ear out for the noisy natterjack toad; in summer, delight in the prettiest butterflies. Take to the waves or the sand, and breathe in the salt-tanged air.

(O) The beach from above; (L) Watersports are a natural choice here; (T) Raven Point Wood; (B) Miles of sandy beach, perfect for leisurely walks

Forth Mountain

Just a couple of miles from Wexford town, Forth Mountain's towering outcrop rises almost 800ft above the land and packs more than just views into an accessible, beautiful hike. Visitors to this overlooked peak will be treated to expansive views of the county, along with the ruins of eighteenth-century cottages and a natural grotto to explore. Lake Carrigfoyle sits at the base of the 'mountain' with clear blue waters and sandy shores, looking more like North America or Italy than southeastern Ireland. Named after the ancient Celtic tribe who once claimed this land, there's history in this earth – from some of the oldest geology to be found in Ireland, over 500 million years in age, to a pivotal battle in the 1798 Rebellion. Also emerging from the ground is new evidence of the 'lost town of Carrig', site of one of the first Norman fortresses in Ireland and a town of over one hundred houses buried and forgotten. Site of the famous Battle of Three Rocks – a major victory for the ultimately unsuccessful United Irishmen of the late eighteenth-century – the rocky slopes of Forth Mountain facilitated a bloody ambush against the British with musket and pike. It's easy to trace the footsteps of those Wexford fighting men along the Three Rocks Trail, taking in the remains of both battle and burial grounds while surrounded by breathtaking views and a wealth of natural delights.

(L) View from the mountain

Johnstown Castle

A 900-hundred-year-old Gothic Revival castle standing proudly on 120 acres, Johnstown Castle is a wonderful piece of Irish history in County Wexford that is worth exploring. Withstanding the test of time in superb order, the castle was fist given to the Esmonde family as a thank you for the role they played in the Norman Invasion of Ireland in 1169. While its towers date back to the 1170s, its neo-Gothic looks came about in the nineteenth century when it was remodelled by the Grogan family. Guided tours of its interior offer a taste of life in bygone times, from the rare servants' tunnel and kitchens to the lavish upstairs quarters. Outside, the ornamental gardens invite serene walks among sculptured topiary and flowers, and summer picnics in the sunken garden. Meander along lakeside paths and through woodland teeming with wildlife. A four-acre walled garden and its hothouses that were first formed in 1844 are being restored to their former splendour. The Irish Agricultural Museum on site explores farming and rural life in wonderful detail.

(L) The castle; (T) Pretty garden trails; (B) The servants' tunnel

Waterford & Tipperary

Waterford and Tipperary balance coast, city history and inland intrigue. Waterford City's Viking and medieval past sits behind workaday quays, while the Greenway, Copper Coast and Ardmore open the county to beaches, cliffs and sea air. Tipperary turns towards the fertile Golden Vale, castle towns and mountain valleys, crowned by the Rock of Cashel, where ecclesiastical ruins rise above pasture with unforgettable authority and remembered power held high in stone.

Coumshingaun Lough

(T) The clear waters of the lake

Here lies a little realm quite literally hidden in the folds of the land. Tucked within steep craggy cliffs on three sides, this paradise is kept off the well-beaten path due to the challenging hike needed to complete it. Just over half an hour's drive from Waterford City, Coumshingaun Lough is easy to find, but difficult to master. The route is three to four hours in total but involves clambering and scrambling over some rough terrain – not to mention coming close to sheer cliffs at times. Climbing up to the plateau and entering the vast gateway of this horseshoe, on a clear day the typically placid waters of the lough will be a mirror filled with mighty cliffs and crags. Up on the ridges await spectacular views of the lake and surrounding country, stretching into infinity on three sides and to the sea on another. A few words of caution, however; good walking equipment, fitness and the ability to navigate are strongly recommended, especially if visibility is affected. Completing the circular route clockwise is also sensible.

Waterford Greenway

A car-free cycle path created along a disused railway line, the Waterford Greenway is one of the country's best car-free cycling and walking paths, encompasing lovely countryside every bit of the way. The 46km-long greenway offers hours of recreational cycling or walking, along Ireland's southeast from Waterford city, through Kilmacthomas and onto the stunning coastal town of Dungarvan. Divided into six sections of varying lengths and difficulty, whichever section you choose, it's a wonderful day out for all fitness levels and ages. Recommended routes for children include the short Killoteran to Kilmeaden section which allows you to hop off and jump on the Suir Valley Heritage train, get great views of the River Suir and drop into lovely Mount Congreve Gardens, or the longer Durrow to Clonee section which takes you through the Ballyvoyle Tunnel, a 400m-long tunnel. The longer sections are more challenging but each section has something to offer, be it a stop at a pub along the way, a Norman castle or a bridge or viaduct with stunning views.

(O) Aerial view of a section of the route running alongside the railway tracks; (L) Inside Ballyvoyle Tunnel; (T) Ballyvoyle Tunnel; (B) Approaching Dungarvan

St Declan's Way

St Declan's Way is the most recent addition to the Pilgrim Paths of Ireland and links Cashel in County Tipperary with Ardmore in County Waterford, both ancient ecclesiastical centres. The 115km route is fully waymarked and follows the route taken by St Declan when going to Cashel to meet St Patrick in the fifth century and has been in use by pilgrims for the past 1500 years to visit St Declan's monastery, holy well and grave in Ardmore. The trail can be split into five stages and goes through mainly flat terrain except for the central section, which takes in the Knockmealdown Mountains, using forest trails and back roads. The surrounding views are mainly of undulating farmland. Along the route you'll pass the Rock of Cashel, reputedly the site of the conversion of Aengus, King of Munster by St Patrick in the fifth century, with current buildings dating from the twelfth and thirteenth centuries, as well as Lismore town with its stunning medieval castle. End in Ardmore, a beautiful seaside village, featuring a cliff walk, ancient round tower and cathedral founded by St Declan, not to mention some great restaurants.

(L) The Round Tower, Ardmore; (T) Following the Way at Ardfinnan; (B) Cahir Castle

Athassel Abbey

The largest medieval priory in the country, twelfth century Athassel Abbey is well off the beaten path and offers the chance to wander alone through 800 years of beautiful history on the banks of River Suir. It was founded by an order of Augustine monks, with the support of William de Burgh, and was dedicated to St Edmund until its dissolution in 1537. Historical and archaeological evidence tells us that the abbey formed the heart of its own urban community at its peak, with perhaps 2000 people coming to live in the surrounding town. A cultural and economic magnet, it attracted attention during times of conflict – resulting in it being burned twice and the town destroyed by the sixteenth century. Set in a verdant four acre site, the priory has been battered and smoothed under the tides of centuries. Though a crumbling stone shell without roof, glass or, in many cases, intact walls, its majesty shines through time. It's clear this place once had the care and love of many monks, attendants, citizens and other clergy who once roamed its hallways, cloisters and gardens. Found in the middle of quiet pastures and usually accessed by hopping a low wall or squeezing through an old gate, Athassel feels like a well-kept secret. You'll likely have nobody but yourself for company in this utterly serene place.

(L) The abbey remains

Rock of Cashel

Viewed from afar, the Rock of Cashel is one of Ireland's great set-piece sights: a solitary limestone outcrop rising above the Golden Vale, crowned by towers, walls, turrets and ecclesiastical ruins. The Rock first rose to prominence as a fortress of Munster's kings, before being granted to the church in the early twelfth century. What remains is a dense and stirring group of medieval buildings, including the round tower, the Gothic cathedral, the Hall of the Vicars Choral and Cormac's Chapel, one of Ireland's most atmospheric Romanesque churches. The site can draw heavy crowds, but the impact of the site survives them. Visit early or late, then take time to look back from the fields around Hore Abbey, where the Rock reveals the full impact of its force. Few places in Ireland express so clearly the old alliance of power, sanctity and landscape.

(L) The view from the abbey's graveyard in the winter; (T) From below; (B) Hore Abbey

Cork & Kerry

Cork and Kerry deliver the southwest at its most varied and compelling, from market city to Atlantic peninsula. Cork has independent spirit, serious food culture, island ports and a coastline that grows wilder towards Mizen, Sheep's Head and Beara. Kerry brings lakes, mountains, Gaeltacht culture, pilgrimage roads and offshore marvels, with Killarney, Dingle, the Blaskets and the Skelligs showing how powerfully landscape can shape memory, language, myth and traveller dreams alike.

CORK
FOOD
IRELAND
www.corkcity.ie
Moynihan
POULTRY
LOIN, HAM & BACON SPECIALIS
SAUSAGES
PUDDING
BODICE
PORK RIB

THE English Market

Food fabulous food, the eighteenth-century English Market slap bang in the middle of Cork city is bursting with mouth-watering stalls that give credence to the city's claim to be the food capital of Ireland. Established in 1788, the attractive red-brick heritage building in which it is housed is a joy to visit in itself with its lofty arched ceiling and airy space. Indeed, this is one of Europe's best covered markets and, oh, is it a sensuous joy to explore. Brimming with artisinal produce, much of which is sourced locally, its fresh and eclectic stalls are a delight. There's seafood caught locally in Ballycotton, cured meats, local cheeses, olives, bread, handmade chocolate, fine pastries, butcher's shops, vegetable stalls, spices and condiments, fine wines, oils, and more. Fill your larder or source a picnic to take to the park or to the sea. Or eat on site, lured in by the tantalising aromas that waft from the delis and stalls.

(L) The market; (T) The freshest of local catches for sale; (B) Fine craft butchers

Spike Island

(T) The remote and eerie Spike Island

Spike Island in Cork Harbour can be reached by taking a ferry from the town of Cobh, a half-hour drive outside of Cork city. An immersive 'augmented reality app' can be used on the island, with fifteen stopping points, enabling visitors to re-live important historical events. The island has a colourful history. It was home to the St Mochuda Monastery (600 AD), followed by a military fortress, later to become the world's largest prison – capable of holding over 2000 inmates – in the 1850s. The prison was used on four separate occasions, in the 1600s, 1800s, during the War of Independence and, most recently, in 1985 as a place to hold young offenders. By taking a tour with a specially trained storyteller you can explore more than twelve museums and exhibitions, prison cells, discreet tunnels, passages and an 1850s punishment block. After this intensive taste of incarceration, it's probably time to get a large dose of fresh air and take yourself off on the Ring of Spike scenic walking trail.

Gougane Barra

It is no exaggeration to say that your first view of St Finbarr's Oratory on the lake at Gougane Barra will take your breath away. Nestled in a valley of the Shehy Mountains, this special place is a haven of peace and tranquillity, where the combination of mountain, lake and forest will calm and refresh the soul. A place of worship was first founded on this site by St Finbarr, patron saint of Cork, in the sixth century on an island in the lake, close to the source of the River Lee. The island is now connected to the shore by a causeway allowing access to the eighteenth-century Oratory which was built near to the site of the original buildings. Nearby are the ruins of a seventeenth-century hermitage which feature stations of the cross. The surrounding hills are home to a 340-acre forest park which has recently seen extensive replanting with native tree species. Choose from six walking trails depending on your fitness level and discover beautiful vistas of the valley as well as waterfalls and gentle river walks. Treat yourself to a stay at the Gougane Barra Hotel, a family-run bolthole which really is a home from home and is right on the lakeshore. Wake up early to catch the mist rising over the water, a magical sight.

(L) The spectacular lake

Glengarriff

Almost as far west in Cork as you can get, just on the border with Kerry, the drive to Glengarriff is almost as enchanting as the end destination. Follow slow, winding roads bordered by mountains and a sea fed by the Gulf Stream, allowing for regular stops for passing sheep, as you journey to this pretty village with its exotic flora and fauna and sparkling blue sea. There is a lot to enjoy here: the sessile oak nature reserve and Pooleen swimming spot, the harbour for sailing and kayaking, gorgeous Garinish Island with its house and Harold Peto Italianate gardens, the Bamboo Park, and Ewe Gallery and Sculpture Garden... Or take to the waters for deep-sea fishing or a marine wildlife tour – and count oyster catchers, egrets, sea eagles, cormorants and grey heron in abundance. On and offshore, the huge colony of harbour seals that calls Glengarriff home is a joy to observe. When the day is done, lunch, dinner or at the very least a drink in the longstanding institution that is The Blue Loo on the Main Street is most definitely a must.

(L) Enjoying sunny days at Harrington's village pub; (T) The gardens on Garinish Island; (B) Ferry to Garnish Island

THE Kerry Way

The 213km-long Kerry Way is a spectacular, circular, waymarked footpath that starts in Killarney, takes in the Muckross Estate, Torc Waterfall, the Upper Lake and the Black Valley before crossing to Glencar, then goes right around the Iveragh Peninsula anticlockwise. Short offshoots head to Glenbeigh, Cahersiveen, Waterville and Caherdaniel, finally passing through Sneem and Kenmare. Mostly following a network of green roads, many of which are old 'butter roads', the route provides magnificent views both of the Iveragh Mountains and of the neighbouring peninsulas, Dingle and Beara. The whole thing can be achieved in nine or ten days, or, with careful study of bus timetables, you could do day-walks along the Way beyond Glenbeigh in summer, or on the section between Glenbeigh and Waterville in winter. Experienced hikers may well be tempted off the Kerry Way to tackle Ireland's highest peak, Carrauntoohil (1038m).

(O) Old Weir Bridge, Killarney Lakes; (L) Torc Waterfall, Killarney; (T) The Kerry Way walking trail

THE Blasket Islands

Just off Slea Head lie the Blaskets, dramatic island mountains with steep, gashed sides. Despite its inhospitable appearance, the largest island, Great Blasket (An Blascaod Mór), was inhabited by up to two hundred people for at least three centuries until 1953, when, with no school, shop, priest or doctor, it was finally abandoned. Because of their isolation, however, the islanders maintained a rich oral tradition in the Irish language, which in the early twentieth century, encouraged by visiting scholars, evolved into a remarkable body of written literature. Works such as *An tOileánach* (The Islandman) by Tomás Ó Criomhthain, *Fiche Blian ag Fás* (Twenty Years A-Growing) by Muiris Ó Súilleabháin and *Peig* by Peig Sayers (an oral account in Irish transcribed by her son) give a vivid insight into the hardships of life there. In the summer, you can take a boat to Great Blasket, or guided cruise around the Blasket Islands, taking in the spectacular Cathedral Rocks on Inishnabro, puffins (in spring and early summer), grey seals and red deer on Inishvickillane (and if you're lucky, basking sharks, whales and dolphins).

(L) Quiet roads and views; (T) Aerial view of the island; (B) Dinghies ferry passengers to boats offshore from the jetty

Killarney National Park

(T) Ross Castle and Lough Leane

Killarney National Park begins almost at the edge of town, but it quickly leaves the resort bustle behind. Its landscape is classic Kerry: three beautiful lakes, wooded shores, glaciated valleys and the dark line of Macgillycuddy's Reeks rising beyond, the highest mountain range in Ireland. The park protects oak, yew and arbutus woods, as well as Ireland's only wild herd of red deer, and there are otters, pine martens, red squirrels and a rich variety of birdlife. It also shelters some of Kerry's best-known historic sights, including Ross Castle (built by the O'Donoghue chieftains in the fifteenth century, with thick bawn walls, corner turrets and a lake-facing tower house positioned to command the waters of Lough Leane), Muckross Friary and Muckross House. The best way in is by moving through it rather than simply stopping for views: by boat from Ross Castle, by bike around Muckross, or on foot towards Torc Waterfall and the lakeshore paths.

Skellig Michael

A voyage to Skellig Michael feels like a journey out of ordinary Ireland altogether. Twelve kilometres off the tip of the Iveragh Peninsula, the larger of the two Skellig islands rises from the Atlantic like a dark tooth of stone, battered by weather and circled by seabirds. On its summit, early medieval monks built a monastery in the late seventh or early eighth century, shaping beehive cells, steps and terraces from the rock in imitation of the desert communities of the early Church. The exposed boat trip, often choppy and entirely dependent on weather, only heightens the sense of arrival. Little Skellig, nearby, is a raucous nature reserve packed with gannets, while Skellig Michael itself remains austere, fragile and extraordinary. Its more recent *Star Wars* fame brought a new audience, but the island's real force lies in its older, established silence.

(L) Walking up to the monastery; (T) The monastery graveyard; (B) A pathway with a view

Dingle Peninsula

The Dingle Peninsula pushes more than 50km into the Atlantic, narrowing towards Slea Head in a superb collision of mountains, sea, surf and stone. Its landscape is unusually varied, from the long beaches of Inch and Castlegregory to the steep slopes of Mount Brandon and the open, ocean-facing roads around the far west. The peninsula is also one of Ireland's richest archaeological landscapes, scattered with dry-stone clocháns, early Christian remains and the beautifully plain Gallarus Oratory, which sits in its field like an upturned boat. This is Corca Dhuibhne, one of the strongest Irish-speaking districts in the country, and Dingle town feels like its busy little capital, with fishing boats, music pubs, restaurants and easy access to the Blaskets. The peninsula rewards lingering. Drive it too fast and you miss the texture – the fields, language, weather, graveyards, sea light, and sudden views.

(O) Dunquin Pier; (L) Inch beach; (T) Shops in Dingle

Limerick & Clare

Across the Shannon, Limerick and Clare offer contrasting pleasures. Limerick city has shaken off old assumptions with museums, markets, rugby pride and a ever-lively cultural pulse, while the county beyond holds archaeological riches and pastoral valleys. Clare is more about the elemental: music towns, monastic islands, the limestone Burren, sea-battered cliffs and a coast lined with golden beaches. This is an area fundamentally defined by Atlantic edge and musical tradition.

Lough Gur

Ireland is overflowing with outstanding archaeological treasures due to its peaty and often waterlogged landscape, making ideal conditions for preserving ancient artefacts and settlements over thousands of years. With so many sites to explore during your time in Ireland, if you had to pick the best? Lough Gur will be near the top of most lists. Scattered along shores, hills and woodlands ringing a magnificent lake, this collection of sites nestled in 'Limerick's Lake District' is an internationally significant archaeological zone. It's home to 136 monuments including Ireland's oldest stone circle, megalithic stone tombs, Bronze and Iron Age crannógs, early Christian hill forts, medieval castles and more. Start at the visitor centre to choose from professional guided tours or self guided trail maps, as well as immersive multimedia exhibitions showcasing 6000 years of Irish history at Lough Gur. From hunter-gathers to the modern human, every step of the Irish people is recorded in this earth. There's something for everyone here, even if standing stones and crumbling fortresses don't get you up in the morning. A fairy trail will have kids diving into the mysteries of this place, while kayaking on the lake is a great way to soak in the ambience.

(L) Aerial view of the stone circle

Craggaunowen

Though the first thing you'll see when you arrive is a resplendent sixteenth century castle turned manor house, the open-air museum that is Craggaunowen in the east of County Clare is focussed further back in Ireland's past – much further. Just beyond the castle, through the veil of trees, emerges a prehistoric Celtic settlement, the crannóg. Surrounded by fifty acres of lush woodland and perched on an ancient man-made island, this award-winning recreation of a Bronze Age Irish ring fort faithfully replicates the exact living conditions and structures of the nation's early inhabitants. Visitors cross into the heart of a lily-covered lake and pass through the fort's single portal into an ancient realm. Join costumed re-enactors spinning wool or making candles among the wide, conical huts and learn about how it was possible to live, fight and thrive in ancient Ireland. Subterranean passageways, Bronze Age industry, stone dolmen tombs and a leather-hulled boat – daringly used to prove the possibility of St Brendan's transatlantic travels in the sixth century – are just some of the treasures to be found here.

(L) The leather-hulled boat; (T) Traditional practices reenactments; (B) The entry to the settlement

Ennistymon

(T) Brightly painted houses are typical in Clare

Ennistymon is located only a few kilometres from County Clare's popular surfy seaside resort of Lahinch, at the doorstep of the Burren, which is why it is sometimes overlooked by visitors hightailing it to the coast. But if you're looking for a great base in the area, Ennistymon is a fantastic option. A market town, the main street has a lot of charming, traditional (and colourful) shopfronts, along with a good selection of pubs, such as Daly's, which is owned by the famous matchmaker, Willie Daly. Food is something you'll definitely want to take time to sample, with freshly baked bread and local cheese, while keen readers will enjoy a riffle through all the books (often in piles) in Banner Books. Lahinch, Doolin, the Cliffs of Moher, the Aran Islands and, of course, the Burren, are all easily reached from Ennistymon. There is a Food and Craft Fair on Sundays, where locally produced goods are sold, and a wander around the stalls provides a great snapshot of the residents of this cosmopolitan town.

Scattery Island

This tiny island is situated at the mouth of the Shannon Estuary, just off the West Clare coastal town of Kilrush. Founded in the sixth century by St Senan, Scattery Island became an important ecclesiastical site for hundreds of years. In 2017 a local family began operating daily boat trips from Kilrush Marina to the island, which quickly gained popularity. It's a short crossing and on arrival during the summer months visitors can enjoy a free tour of the main sites, including the remains of the monastic settlement, the cathedral and the five churches, as well as the deserted village, large round tower and a holy well. There are two walking trails on the island, one of which brings you to the working lighthouse and a Napoleonic artillery battery. A small visitor centre in a restored cottage tells the history of island life through the years until 1978 when the last inhabitant left. When back on the mainland, in the proximity of Kilrush town is a Dolphin and Wildlife Centre, Museum of Irish Rural Life and the superb Vandeleur Walled Garden, an impeccably maintained botanic garden with pleasant woodland walks and bistro.

(L) Monastic relics; (T) The shape of the island; (B) Resting by the visitor centre

Mullaghmore Mountain

The Burren (Bhoireann in Irish) is one of the most unique areas in Ireland. It has the appearance of a 'Lunar landscape' but don't be deceived, there is an abundance of exotic plants to be discovered in the stark limestone rock, especially orchids. The Burren contains many castles, ancient churches, large stately homes and ancient wedge tombs spread throughout the region. No visit to the Burren is complete without a trip to Mullaghmore Mountain, however. Travel down a country road from the village of Kilnaboy and a hulking rocky tabletop suddenly comes into view. After a short distance down a small track, a closer vantage point allows you to admire the dramatic layered shape with the small Lough Gealain at its base. You immediately become aware why Mullaghmore is called a sacred mountain. The Burren National Park is here and a looped trail can be taken right to the top of Mullaghmore, for views of the dramatic limestone surroundings. Fans of *Father Ted* are in luck, too, because the 'Parochial House' used for filming is nearby.

(O) An otherworldly, stark mountain plateau; (L) Natural flora; (T) Cycling through the vast lunar landscape; (B) The famed Parochial House

Cliffs of Moher

The Cliffs of Moher form one of Ireland's most famous edges, dropping almost 200m into the Atlantic in a long, battered line south of Doolin. Their popularity is no mystery. On a clear day, the views stretch out towards the Aran Islands, Galway Bay and the mountains of Connemara, while the cliff faces themselves shift with weather and light, sometimes black and severe, sometimes bright with seabirds and spray. O'Brien's Tower marks the classic viewpoint, but the cliffs are best appreciated by walking a little distance from the busiest areas, where the scale begins to register and the sound of the ocean rises from below. They also make sense of the surrounding landscape: Doolin to the north, Lahinch to the south, and the Burren behind. For all the visitor-centre bustle, the cliffs remain elemental, exhilarating and faintly unnerving.

(L) Hiking by the cliff edge

ARAN KNITWEAR
Village Crafts
The Sweater Shop
OPEN

Doolin

Doolin began its modern fame as a traditional music village, associated above all with the Russell brothers, whose singing, flute and whistle playing drew enthusiasts here from the 1960s onwards. The village is much busier now, and its pubs often fill with visitors, but its position remains hard to beat. It sits just north of the Cliffs of Moher, close to the Burren's limestone pavements, and its pier is one of the main gateways to the Aran Islands. This makes Doolin less a single sight than a gathering point for several strands of western Ireland: music, sea crossings, cliff walks, caves, stone walls and wind-bent fields. The best visits avoid treating it as a box to tick. Instead, stay long enough for the evening pace to settle in, walk down towards the harbour, and Doolin's older appeal – as part village, part outpost – begins to shine through.

(O) The village; (L) Doolin Ferry company;
(T) Traditional music at Gus O'Connors pub

Galway

Galway is the west in concentrated form, lively, salty and restless, with a city that seems to lean towards the sea. Its streets are filled with music, festivals, students, food and Irish-language echoes, while beyond them Connemara breaks into mountains, bogs, lakes and Atlantic islands. The Arans, Killary, Dog's Bay and Letterfrack reveal a landscape both rough and luminous, where culture and weather feel inseparable from everyday life.

Killary Fjord

(T) Views from the deck

Board the catamaran *Connemara Lady* at Nancy's Point pier, 2km west of Leenane village, and glide along Ireland's only glacial fjord enjoying some spectacular Connemara scenery. The Killary Fjord is 14km-long with a width ranging from 42 to 700m. On one side the landscape has ice age terraces in the form of Ordovician gritstones, shales and volcanic rocks, while the other has a special type of reef composed of Silurian sandstone and mudstone. Over the years this area has attracted many writers and artists to stay and work, among them Oscar Wilde and painter Paul Henry. During the voyage, a running commentary through loudspeakers (heard best on the outside decks) gives interesting details about the geology and history of the area. As the fjord is well sheltered, you can expect calm sailing conditions to generally apply. Highly recommended for a leisurely boat trip or for the more adventurous, kayaking and diving.

Letterfrack

Founded in 1849 by a Quaker family, the story of Letterfrack is a harrowing chapter in Irish history due to the horrific and tragic events that unfolded in St Joseph's Industrial School for boys from 1887, and up until it closed in 1974. The former Christian Brothers institution was plagued with physical and sexual abuse, and a hillside graveyard in the village is littered with marble headstones commemorating seventy-nine named children who died while attending the industrial school. Post 1974, everything changed for the better in Letterfrack when members of the local community purchased the old school and a whole new era began. It now houses several excellent community-based projects. In 1980 the government established the Connemara National Park, which unfurls beside the village. It is home to an official Poetry Trail – one of only two in the West of Ireland. Poems are displayed on special plaques at different locations, all written by well-known Irish poets with the theme 'celebrating the importance of place'. Some are general in nature; others deal with the area's troubled history.

(L) The village is nestled beside Diamond Hill mountain; (T) A scenic wonderland surrounds the village; (B) Poetic plaques

Connemara National Park

The Connemara National Park covers a thin slice of the northwest sector of the Twelve Bens, stretching east as far as Benbrack, Bencullagh, Muckanaght and Benbaun. It includes an excellent walkway to the top of Diamond Hill (about 2hr 30min return). The path starts at the visitor centre and the 8km route follows the Sruffaunboy Nature Trail before branching off towards the cone of Diamond Hill. From the cairn on the summit ridge at 442m high the breathtaking view embraces islands, bays, beaches, loughs and mountains. There are three shorter nature trails across the lower slopes, through some natural woodland and over bogland, with free guided walks on Wednesday and Friday mornings in July and August. The park's visitor centre contains a fascinating exhibition on the wildlife and geology of Connemara and a café. There's also a children's playground. From here you can easily take in Letterfrack on the same day for its lovely Poetry Trail.

(O) Natural habitats for the park's flora and fauna abound; (L) The prettiest mountain streams; (T) Follow Irish legend and seek a pot of gold at the end of a rainbow; (B) The park at dusk

Dog's Bay Beach

Soft white sand on a sheltered horseshoe bay that stretches for 1.5km... Dog's Bay Beach in County Galway is one of the prettiest beaches in Ireland. Indeed, on a fine day you'd be forgiven for imagining you were far from the bracing bite of the Atlantic Ocean. The slim strip of dunes that separates it from Gurteen Beach has, as in many coastal areas, been planted with Marram grass in a bid to prevent coastal erosion. Take to the beach year-round for a walk or lay out the towels in summer. Swimming is possible here, too, but there are no lifeguards on duty so caution is advised. Afterwards, drive the short 2km to the lovely fishing village of Roundstone where you can dine in O'Dowd's Seafood Bar and Restaurant, enjoying the freshest catch of the day – think hake, haddock, mussels, crab and lobster, hearty chowder and meaty mains, all in a traditional Irish pub setting, perhaps accompanied by a pint of Guinness or a glass of wine.

(L) Beach perfection in Galway

www.galwayoysterfest.com
GATOR

Galway Oyster Festival

The Galway Oyster Festival is one of Europe's longest-running food festivals and has been drawing people to County Galway for over 64 years. So why are these oysters so celebrated? It's a debatable topic but some would say it is the perfect harvesting conditions that give them an unrivalled taste – a combination of the sheltered setting and the Atlantic, mixed with the sweet notes derived from the limestone in the Burren and the smoky, peaty flavour of the Connemara bogs. The festival celebrates the first oyster harvest of the season with gusto, offering a programme of music, delicious seafood, cookery demos, parade, and of course, the Guinness World Oyster Opening Championship (each competitor must open thirty of the molluscs as quickly as possible and present them perfectly on a tray). Wash down your oysters with a pint of Guinness, the unofficial beverage of choice. Alternatively, there is no shortage of champagne, fine wine or indeed any other tipple of your choice. Not big on oysters? Don't worry. The atmosphere and craic alone make this one not to miss.

(L) The Oyster Opening Championship; (T) A lovely pairing – Guinness and oysters; (B) An important announcement

Inis Mór

The largest of the Aran Islands, Inis Mór is an otherworldly eruption of rugged limestone jutting out into the squalls and storms of the Atlantic, on the very western edge of Europe. This ancient land holds evidence of prehistoric habitation as far back as 3000 BC, and today remains home to 900 hardy and deeply Irish souls. While just forty minutes from the mainland by ferry, the farthest of these famous islands feels a world apart from – at times – Earth itself. The island's jagged coastlines, sea-scraped limestone plateaus and mysterious, ancient clifftop forts feel straight out of an interstellar sci-fi blockbuster or fantasy epic. Humans have a foothold on this island but will always share it with the sea and its creatures. The bizarre wormhole (known as the 'Serpent's Lair') is a naturally formed and almost perfectly rectangular pool sliced out of the base of the cliffs, seemingly carved by the hand of some ancient ocean god. Beware entering, however, as its waters are fed through underground caves and can drain in the blink of an eye – or suddenly rage with a great Atlantic swell.

(L) The rugged cliff-face; (T) Uncrowded beaches are a given; (B) Ancient fort

Mayo

Mayo feels spacious, underpopulated and quietly intense, a county of pilgrim mountains, broad bays, dark skies and islands at the edge of things. Westport projects comfort and elegance beneath Croagh Patrick, while Newport, Clare Island and Achill draw you towards emptier horizons. In the north, bogland and ancient field systems deepen the sense of remoteness, underlining the sense of Mayo as truly undiscovered, and all the stronger for it.

Newport

Newport, a heritage town located on the shores of Clew Bay in County Mayo along the Wild Atlantic Way, has many interesting places to explore. The town's centrepiece is the Victorian red stone railway viaduct with seven arches (in operation from 1894-1937). There is also an abbey, ancient wood ringfort, plus the last stained-glass window designed by world-famous artist Harry Clarke in the local church. Another big attraction is seeing the ancestral home of actress Grace Kelly, later to become Princess Grace of Monaco. Grace Kelly's paternal grandfather, John, hailed from a small thatched cottage a couple of kilometres from Newport. He emigrated to Philadelphia in 1887, where he went on to found a major construction company. As Princess Grace of Monaco, the former Hollywood star made several visits to the town during the sixties and seventies; there are several photos of these visits in the local tourist information office. On her last stay she examined plans to build a holiday home on the site of her grandfather's home. However, this never reached fruition as she died following a car accident a couple of years later. Newport has two hotels, Irish music pubs and several cafés. Be sure to drop into Kelly's artisan butchers' shop, winners of numerous awards for dry cured rashers, sausages and both black and white puddings.

(L) The bridge into town

Mayo Dark Sky Park

In 2016 the Mayo Dark Sky Park was officially launched following a submission sent to the International Dark-Sky Association based in Arizona and accepted. It was designated as Gold Tier, the highest possible accolade. There are just one hundred such parks around the world. As a follow up, it was decided to hold an annual festival here. If you enjoy looking at, or have a particular interest in, the night sky then the Mayo Dark Sky Festival, held each November, is a must-do. While the festival takes place mainly around Wild Nephin National Park, several events over the weekend are held in neighbouring towns of Newport and Mulranny. There are always lots of activities such as torchlight walks, science workshops, a mobile planetarium and, of course, stargazing. Many well-known names in the fields of science and night sky photography regularly attend. However, any time of the year is good to visit this unspoilt region consisting of the Nephin Beg Range and Owenbeg bog, the last intact blanket bog system in Ireland and Western Europe.

(O) Perfect stargazing conditions; (L) St Patrick's Church, Newport; (T) Starry splendour; (B) The aurora borealis

Clare Island

Rugged and mountainous, Clare Island stands guard at the entry of Clew Bay. Always in sight from the shores of County Mayo and shrouded in mystery, this little land is home to the tomb of a pirate queen, numerous Bronze Age sites and old sailors' pubs frozen in time. Most travellers hop over on a daytrip before ploughing on, or bypass it altogether, but Clare Island will reward patient travellers who give it more of their time. It has an atmosphere of its own, sparsely populated and ringed with towering cliffs, but doesn't lack in golden-sanded beaches and peaceful woodlands. Claimed in the sixteenth century by the Ó Máille dynasty and its pirate queen, who controlled the seas of Connacht from this hardy outpost, it formed the setting for Michael Morpurgo's award-winning children's novel, *The Ghost of Grania O'Malley*. Get swept up in the legend of the pirate queen before arriving or while you're there, exploring the peaceful island and enjoying its fresh air with few other souls, if any, for company. A number of excellent holiday homes, including the majestic lighthouse itself, make it a great base for a true getaway.

(O) The lighthouse; (T) An inviting cycle trail; (B) The harbour and Gráinne O'Malleys castle (spellings of her name vary)

Keem Bay

(T) The prettiest bay

A secluded beach hidden on an island, with golden sand and crystal blue water, ringed by green cliffs and offering incredible views? Not heaven, but almost. This one-of-a-kind spot is found on Achill Island, the largest isle in the country, which sits at one of the westernmost points of Europe. Catch Keem Bay on a sunny day and you could be forgiven for thinking you've stumbled across the Atlantic and into the Caribbean. The beach is located at the bottom of a deep, horseshoe bay, giving it great protection from the elements and a wonderful sense of seclusion. With a Blue Flag certification for cleanliness, the utterly clear waters here are perfect for taking in the marine life of the wild west coast by swimming, diving and snorkelling. Keem Bay is accessed just off the Wild Atlantic Way, requiring a jaw-dropping detour to reach. Taking a guided kayak tour of the island will give you a chance to explore the other stretches of coastline that Achill Island has to offer, combined with fishing and other watersports.

Sligo, Leitrim & Roscommon

Sligo, Leitrim and Roscommon are bound together by music, water and old stories. Sligo's coast and mountains carry the charge of Yeats, with Benbulben, Lough Gill and ancient cemeteries giving the county an unmistakable profile. Leitrim is quieter, threaded by lakes, canals and the Shannon. Roscommon, often overlooked, is rich in atmosphere and rewards slow exploration. Travelling here on inland backroads share glimpses of royal sites, mining memories, ruined towns and big-house history.

Yeats Country

Fondly known as Yeats Country, it was Sligo that captured the heart of one of Ireland's most acclaimed poets. Born in Dublin in 1865, William Butler Yeats spent much of his life in Drumcliffe where his grandfather was the rector at the village church. You can visit his grave in the cemetary at Drumcliffe Church which overlooks Benbulbin, a final resting place requested in his poem Under Ben Bulben. Benbulbin itself is an imposing verdant summit in the Dartry Mountains in County Sligo, close to the border with County Leitrim. It's bursting with interesting flora and fauna and presents a moderate to demanding 8km hiking trail up to the peak and back that rewards with its dramatic views over Donegal Bay. From here, an alternate and easier trail is the 50-minute walk to see the Devil's Chimney. Standing at 492ft, it is Ireland's tallest waterfall. Another of its quirks is that it's only visible after a spout of rainfall, thankfully not often an issue given Ireland's climate. Nearby is also popular Glencar Waterfall.

(O) Benbulbin's dramatic setting; (L) Countryside befitting a poet; (T) The Devil's Chimney waterfall; (B) W B Yeats' grave in Drumcliffe

Coney Island

The original Coney Island, it was this sand-laced speck off Strandhill in County Sligo that gave its American counterpart its name, or so the story goes. Vastly different in appearance, there are no fairground attractions here, just a few kilometres of beach in an unspoilt location. Legend has it that the sea captain of a nineteenth-century merchant ship Arethusa who sailed the route from Sligo to New York, having taken note of the large number of rabbits in New York, decided to name the American neighbourhood after his own island off the Coolera peninsula in Sligo – the word 'Coney' coming from the Irish word coinín (pronounced quin-neen) for rabbit. A cute story, whether there is any truth to it or not. To get here you can hop on a boat from Rosses Point or follow the more fun driving route waymarked by fourteen stone pillars from Cummeen Strand for 5km – accessible at low tide only. Come spend a few hours on uncrowded, pristine beaches, enjoy a spot of surfing or a dip in the sea, then saunter in for a pint in the island's only pub, McGowans. Just make sure to time your return with the tide or you'll be stopping overnight.

(L) Beach on Coney Island

River Shannon Blueway

Turn off from the Wild Atlantic Way coast road and you'll find many paths less travelled. The River Shannon Blueway is one such network of biking and hiking trails, weaving around the many lakes, canals and rivers of Leitrim. A county that got its first traffic lights in 2016, it offers an excellent break from travelling by car – explore a number of unspoiled landscapes by foot and bike on land, or cruise the waterways by kayak, canoe or stand-up paddleboard. Dotted with excellent restaurants and gastropubs, the Shannon Blueway's well-fed travellers can glide through nearly 50km of fields, forests and fallen ruins from Drumshanbo to the tip of Lough Ree. You can just rock up to any of the many entry points for a short walking loop, guided paddle, or to relax by the water. A host of quaint villages and waterside towns will greet you, each suffused with its own blend of raucous pubs, musical communities and historical oddities.

(O) Boardwalk over the Blueway;
(L) Woodland walking trails; (T) Exploring by kayak

Arigna Mines

Arigna was Ireland's last working coal mine, in use from the 1700s to the 1990s. Located amid the beautiful scenery of Lough Allen, the surrounding land was not well suited to agriculture and so coal mining provided a valuable income for local people. The mine has been impressively repurposed with strong local community support into a valuable and fascinating insight into the working lives of miners, while the unique visitor centre was designed to resemble a coal slag heap. Tours into the mine are run by ex-miners who provide a wealth of first-hand knowledge and experience. The exhibition area features historical documents, photographs and early mining equipment, bringing to life nearly four hundred years of mining history. A short film also captures footage of mining taking place just before the closure of the mine. Following your visit, you could stretch your legs by taking a walk along the Miner's Way and Historical trail, a 118km-long network of paths stretching into Roscommon's neighbouring counties of Leitrim and Sligo. Then quench your thirst in the Miners Bar in Arigna.

(L, T) In the mines; (B) Machinery used for mining

Rathcroghan

Although it is one of the most important historical and mythological sites in Ireland, Rathcroghan in County Roscommon is often overlooked in favour of more developed attractions. The complex encompasses hundreds of archaeological sites including ringforts, burial mounds and standing stones, spanning 5500 years of human history. It was the home of Medb, Queen of Connacht, and is an integral part of the Táin Bó Cúailnge epic. The sites are largely unexcavated, and many are located on private land, therefore a tour run by the Rathcroghan Visitor Centre is highly recommended. This will also include a visit to the evocative Oweynagat Cave, entrance to 'the Underworld' or the 'Gates of Hell'. Legend has it that during Samhain (the festival marking the beginning of winter and starting on 31 October) the underworld would open and beasts and monsters could enter the world of the living. In order to protect themselves, local people would dress in ghoulish disguises to fool the demons, thus the tradition of dressing up for Halloween.

(O) One of the mounds; (L) Inside Oweynagat Cave – the 'Gates of Hell'; (T) The Rathcroghan complex; (B) Informative panels in the Visitor Centre

Rindoon Medieval Town

(T) The remains of Rindoon

On the Warrenpoint peninsula lies the deserted medieval town of Rindoon, regarded as an unparalleled set of ruins, and yet almost entirely undisturbed since its abandonment centuries ago. The Norman-era ruins include a town wall, castle, hospital, church and mill. Undeveloped as a tourist attraction, your only company will most likely be some grazing cattle. A looped walk will take you around the peninsula, taking in beautiful views across Lough Ree. A short stroll away, on the western shores of Lough Ree near the village of Lecarrow, St John's Wood is one of Ireland's largest surviving ancient woodlands, an incredibly valuable habitat and a reminder of what much of the landscape would have looked like before massive deforestation. It forms part of Lough Ree Special Area of Conservation. The wood's age and lack of disturbance has led to wonderful biodiversity, providing shelter to pine martens, wood warblers and flowers such as the bird's-nest orchid. The wild cherry tree is also particularly common.

Strokestown House

An impressive Palladian mansion, Strokestown House was owned by the same family (the Mahons) for over three hundred years. It is best known for housing the National Famine Museum, which details both the local history of the Park's aristocratic landlords and their tenants, as well as the larger national factors which contributed to the Great Irish Famine in the mid-nineteenth century. The house itself is a beautiful example of Georgian architecture and the tour provides insight into the lives of the gentry and servants, as both the grand rooms and the kitchens and servants' quarters are open to view. Outside are six acres of walled gardens which include one of Ireland's longest herbaceous borders, a fernery and a Victorian rose garden. The surrounding woodland offers family-friendly trails and a number of ancient beech and oak trees. Original garden machinery is on display and a refurbished glasshouse gives a glimpse into how the estate gardens were managed to provide food for the 'big house'. Here, a vivid picture emerges of the parallel lives of rich and poor during that terrible period in Irish history.

(O) The grand facade; (T) In the opulent dining room; (B) Displays inside the musuem

Donegal

Donegal feels magnificently apart, cut off by geography and sharpened by weather, with some of Ireland's richest scenery along its indented coast. Sea cliffs, headlands, islands, beaches, bogs and mountains create a county of fierce contrasts, from Slieve League to Inishowen and Tory. Inland, Glenveagh and the hills around Errigal add grandeur, while Irish-speaking districts keep local culture close to the land, with the Atlantic always present, never too far away.

Malin Head

(T) The dramatic Atlantic coastline

The northernmost outpost of Ireland, Malin Head is the Republic at its most elemental, an exhilaratingly remote landscape providing respite from the white noise of modernity. On offer are beautiful beaches and mighty sand dunes, gusty clifftop walks, and premier-class flora and fauna. Birding is big news here, with a healthy population of choughs populating the cliffs, while between October and March, the fields teem with thousands of Greenland barnacle geese chomping incessantly off the rich pasture. Check out the view from Banba's Crown, a storm-lashed promontory, topped by a ruined Napoleonic signal tower, from where a path heads out to Hell's Hole, a 75m chasm in the cliffs pounded by the onrushing tide. From the Head's many blustery vantage points, there are some fine vistas, including Fanad Head Lighthouse and Tory Island to the west, and the Scottish island of Islay over to the northwest. Get your timings right and you may even catch a glimpse of the Northern Lights.

Slieve League

A magical masterpiece of nature, the Slieve League (Sliabh Liag) – one of the most spectacular sections of the Wild Atlantic Way, a coastal strip that runs for 1600 miles along Ireland's western seaboard – remains a relatively little-visited part of the Republic. This is somewhat surprising given that these are some of the highest sea cliffs anywhere in Europe, standing at a whopping 1972ft or double the height of the Eiffel Tower. The Slieve serves up some terrific walks, from the easy – such as the 45-minute trek to the Bunglass Point viewpoint – to the short but tough Pilgrim's Path, an outing really only suited to seasoned hikers. Those with a head for heights might like to test their mettle on its extension, the One Man's Pass (the clue is in the name), a thrilling, knife-edge walk along a track high above the Atlantic. Reaching the summit of Slieve League, you'll be rewarded with an out look as memorable as anywhere on the Emerald Isle.

(O) One Man's Pass; (L) A natural outdoor playground for the intrepid; (T) The best views reward those who hike the trail

Tory Island

Buffeted by seething Atlantic waves nine miles off the northwest coast of Donegal, Tory Island is Ireland's remotest inhabited island. Small it may be, but the island and its Gaelic-speaking residents – all 150 of them squeezed onto a wedge of rock just three miles by one – is thriving; it's now even got its own school. A resilient and welcoming bunch, Tory Islanders will guarantee first-class hospitality to any visitor, which extends to opening the doors to all-comers for evenings of Gaelic storytelling and ceilidhs, held all year round. Not that Tory's residents are particularly inclined to making concessions to modern-day visitors' busy timetables – you have been warned... Above all else, the island is renowned for its primitive, or naïve, landscape painters, a small coterie of artists who emerged in the 1960s, led by the English painter Derek Hill. The latter went on to influence the likes of James Dixon, a crofter and fisherman whose former home is now a gallery where a small but fascinating record of Tory Island life over fifty years is beautifully documented.

(L) Aerial view of the inhabited island; (T) Quaint island houses; (B) Unspoilt beaches

Glenveagh Castle

Glenveagh Castle was built on a small promontory for wealthy landowner George Adair between 1870 and 1873. The rhododendron-filled gardens surrounding the castle were very much the work of Adair's wife, Cornelia, who also introduced herds of red deer to the estate. The steep ascent to the viewpoint behind the gardens is more than worthwhile for the wonderful views down to the castle and along the lough deep into the glen in Glenveagh National Park. The Poisoned Glen – east of Dunlewey Lough, is one of the most popular spots of the park. Overall, it's easy to imagine why the castle was so popular during the Golden Age of Hollywood, with Greta Garbo, Marilyn Monroe and Clark Gable all spending time here. Guided tours of the castle focus on the furniture and artwork collected by the millionaire Irish–American, Henry McIlhenny, the last owner of Glenveagh. The Glenveagh National Park Visitor Centre has detailed and interactive displays on the area's ecology and geology, and on the park's wildlife, in particular its eagles.

(O) Aerial view of the castle and its gardens; (L) The castle; (T) Grand interiors; (B) Dunlewey Lough

Grianán OF Aileach

The Grianán of Aileach stands high on a hilltop above the Inishowen Peninsula, a restored circular stone fort with some of the finest views in Donegal. From its ramparts, the landscape falls away towards Lough Swilly, Lough Foyle, the Inishowen hills and, on a clear day, deep into neighbouring counties. The site's origins are ancient, and though the present walls were heavily restored in the nineteenth century, the sense of old power remains intact. It is the setting that makes the place unforgettable. You climb through the entrance into a ring of dry stone, then up the internal steps to look out over a landscape of water, fields and distant mountains. Unlike more elaborate historic sites, Grianán does not need much interpretation. Its purpose is immediately legible: command, ritual, defence, display. Few hillforts in Ireland make landscape feel so much like authority.

(L) The Fort

LOYAL AND DEVOTED WORKMEN
NAVAL ARCHITECT
GUSTAV WOLFF

Antrim & Derry

Antrim and Derry combine dramatic coast, urban memory and some of Northern Ireland's strongest cultural landmarks. Antrim's shore road curls past glens, villages, cliff paths and basalt wonders, with the Giant's Causeway and Rathlin giving it mythic force. Derry brings a different intensity: intact walls, contested streets, murals, museums and the legacy of Seamus Heaney, all set against a hinterland of strands, fields and low hills, with history pressing close.

BELFAST'S Linen Quarter

Belfast's emergence as a bona fide tourist destination owes much to the regeneration of the Linen Quarter, so-named from the time when Belfast could lay fair claim to being the linen capital of the world, an industry that played a pivotal role in the city's social and economic development during the nineteenth century. Many of the quarter's distinctive red brick warehouses remain, one of which is now the Linen Hall Library, the oldest in Belfast and whose archives are second to none. Peruse, too, the display of political posters as you head up the stairwell towards the café. Worth investigating also is the Linen Quarter's musical heritage, whether it's a performance at the prestigious Grand Opera House, a classical soirée at the Ulster Hall (Charles Dickens once read here) or some head-throbbing rock at the legendary Limelight club; not forgetting, either, Fibber McGee's, which hosts Irish music seven days a week. Last word, however, goes to The Crown Liquor Saloon, a timeless Victorian gin palace that is emphatically one not to be missed (see page 192).

(O) Performance at Ulster Hall; (L) The Grand Opera House; (T) Linen Hall Library; (B) Aerial view of Belfast

THE Crown Liquor Saloon

(T) The fabulous interior

Taking pride of place in the very centre of Belfast, this perfectly preserved and opulent Victorian 'gin palace' offers a drinking experience like no other. The Crown Liquor Saloon's exquisite features remain frozen in time since the nineteenth century, when Italian craftsmen working on local churches were directed towards the creation of an alternative place of solace, comfort and beauty in the 1880s. A lavish drinking establishment, fit for its fashionable patrons, emerged in a riot of kaleidoscopic tiles, stained-glass and ornate wood panelling. Today you'll find a chance to tip back a glass in much the same way customers have been for over a hundred years. Heated footrests sit underneath a massive granite-topped bar, studded with imposing ale casks and Neoclassical columns, while ten private booths with latched doors allow drinkers to imbibe away from prying eyes. Take a seat in one and you'll find gunmetal panels for striking matches and antique ringing bells for summoning (non-antique) bar staff.

...OUR REVENGE WILL BE THE LAUGHTER OF OUR CHILDREN
EVERYONE, REPUBLICAN OR OTHERWISE HAS THEIR OWN PARTICULAR ROLE TO PLAY
Bobby Sands MP
POET, GAEILGEOIR, REVOLUTIONARY, IRA VOLUNTEER

Belfast Political Tour

The Troubles is a definitive period in Northern Irish history. This conflict – a war to some – drew its fuel across nationality, politics and religion, plaguing the country and its neighbours for several decades. There are few residents of Belfast who haven't been impacted by it in some way; its scars are visible to this day, with 26km of peace walls still dividing neighbourhoods and many locals living with broken families, friends lost or painful memories. The Belfast Political Tour (www.belfastpoliticaltour.com) is a chance to get a real glimpse of this turbulent period and the stories of those involved. Led and delivered by ex-political prisoners from both sides, they'll let you see through their eyes and feel what they felt as they risked imprisonment, injury or death for their beliefs. Weaving through the streets and landmarks of the city, it's an undeniably unique and visceral, immediate experience. One guide will pass you over to another through a gate in the peace wall at the tour's mid-point, tactfully combining the history and humanity of what is still recent, raw and not entirely resolved for the people of Belfast.

(L) A memorial to Bobby Sands; (T) The tour on Bombay Street; (B) Falls Road murals

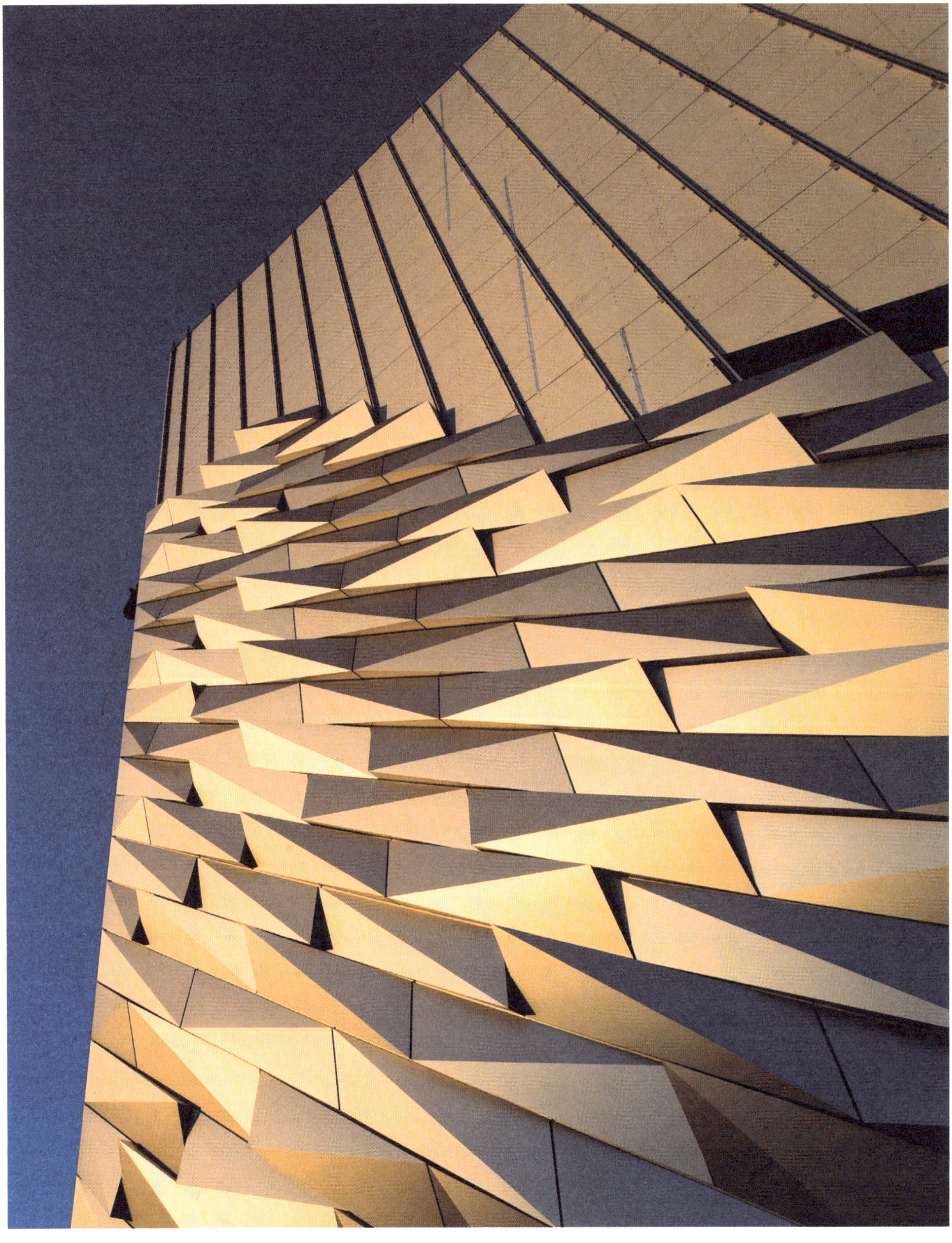

Titanic Quarter

History famously recollects that the RMS *Titanic* was built here at the Harland & Wolff shipyard in east Belfast between 1909 and 1912, and sank just four days into her maiden voyage, on 12 April 1912. It's a story that is memorably recalled in Titanic Belfast, the centrepiece of the Titanic Quarter, one of Europe's largest urban waterfront regeneration projects. A stunning prow-like structure (at 38m – the same height as the ship's hull) clad with some three thousand silver-anodised aluminium shards, it's an inspiring testament to both the doomed ship and the city that built it. The highlight is a shipyard experience ride that sees passengers travel through the sights and sounds of Harland & Wolff as it circumnavigates a replica of the ship's rudder during construction. There's more to the Titanic Quarter than just big ships, though: it's home to the *Game of Thrones* trail, a series of stained-glass installations dotted along the Maritime Mile.

(O) The Titanic Quarter; (L) SS Nomadic, a former tender of the White Star line; (T) The exhibition hall at Titanic Belfast

Cave Hill

Cave Hill is Belfast's great natural lookout, rising above the city to the north with Belfast Lough spread below and the streets gathered tight around the river. For visitors, it offers the simplest way to grasp the shape of the capital: the docklands, the hills, the sweep of water, the hard industrial geography that made the city. The climb also gives Belfast a welcome change of rhythm. After the bars, museums and political tours, the paths up Cave Hill lead through open slopes and rougher ground towards the basalt crags that dominate the skyline. Its most famous feature, known as Napoleon's Nose, has long been said to have helped inspire Jonathan Swift's image of the sleeping giant in *Gulliver's Travels*. Whether or not you buy the story, the hill has a mythic quality of its own, guarding Belfast from above while keeping it firmly in view.

(L) View from the top

THE Gobbins

Chiselled into the base of a cliff face on the eastern flank of the long, banana-shaped Islandmagee peninsula, the Gobbins is an unforgettable 3km-long walkway tracing the Atlantic coastline. Derived from the Gaelic gobán, meaning 'headland', the Gobbins was originally conceived by railway engineer Berkeley Deane Wise in 1902 in an attempt to lure a new class of Edwardian visitor to the area. Eventually closed in 1960, it reopened in 2015. Kitted out with a hard hat, you're bussed down to the start of the path, which begins at a viewing point affording tremendous views of the sea-bitten coastline and the faint hump of Ailsa Craig just off the Ayrshire coast. The walk proper begins at Wise's Eye, a diminutive tunnel bored into the rock face; thereafter, the new 3km-long path roughly tracks Wise's original, albeit now almost totally eroded, version, running through a series of dramatic tunnels, staircases and suspension bridges. The birdlife here is first-class: kittiwakes, guillemots, razorbills and puffins cling precariously to the cliff ledges, while gannets spear headfirst into the North Channel's foamy waters.

(L) The dramatic walkway; (T) An adrenaline-fuelled walk above the Atlantic; (B) The Gobbins cliff path

Giant's Causeway

Some say that it was the legendary Irish giant Fionn mac Cumhall (or Fin McCool) who carved out the Giant's Causeway in order to reach Scotland to fight his Celtic nemesis Benandonner. Others maintain that it was Bernandonner himself who built the walkway before tearing it up as he fled in terror after being tricked into mistaking the disguised Fionn for his giant baby son – nice stories both, but the more prosaic reality was that this marvel of nature was formed as a result of a volcanic eruption some sixty million years ago, which left the molten basalt to cool into the remarkable rock formations we see today: some 40,000 upright hexagonal basalt columns standing like soldiers on sentry. As Northern Ireland's classic travel icon – and sole UNESCO World Heritage Site – the Causeway constantly bristles with visitors, but there are ways to avoid the hordes. The catch is, you'll have to walk there (though by doing so you avoid the expensive car park fee), which is no hardship, especially if you approach it along the Causeway Coast Way, which stretches for some 51km between Ballycastle in the east to Portstewart in the west. Highlights en route include Dunluce Castle, the vertigo-inducing Carrick-a-Rede rope bridge, and a wee stop at The Bushmills Inn, whose whiskey has been distilled there since 1608, giving it the proud distinction of being the world's oldest licenced distillery.

(L) The basalt causeway

Rathlin Island

Almost as close to the Mull of Kintyre in Scotland as it is to Ballycastle on the Irish mainland, the boot-shaped Rathlin Island is Northern Ireland's only inhabited island, yet despite its proximity to the mainland, Rathlin feels gloriously remote. It's a wild, craggy place with a coastline consisting almost entirely of limestone and basalt cliffs that rise some 200ft out of the Atlantic, and fields sheathed in blankets of wild orchids and banks of primroses. Rathlin offers much by way of real escape, not least outstanding birdlife, being home to one of the largest seabird colonies in Ireland, including fulmars, guillemots, razorbills and gannets, numbers swollen in spring by thousands of puffins. Factor in some terrific hiking and biking, locally caught seafood in the Manor House hotel, and creamy pints of Guinness and traditional music in McCuaig's Bar, and you're all set. A great time to visit is the end of May for the Rathlin Sound Maritime Festival, a week-long jamboree of nautically themed events, the highlight of which is the Blessing of the Boats ceremony.

(O) Rathlin West Lighthouse, a beacon for ships on a foggy night; (L) An island viewing point; (T) Have a pint of the black stuff in McCuaigs; (B) Abandoned cottage at Usher Point

Portstewart Strand

(T) The wide expanse that is Portstewart Strand

A glorious 3km stretch of sand firm enough to drive on – which many folk do – the National Trust-owned Portstewart Strand is so wide that you never feel crowded out. For the more active-minded, there's a fairly easy four-mile walk beginning at the Portstewart Visitor Centre, which takes you through age-old dunes dusted with tufts of pale green grasses, then down to the Bann estuary, where the path follows the river's edge and returns to the golden beach. Portstewart also offers some of the best surfing in the country: operating out of a van at the entrance to the car park, the friendly folk at Ocean Warriors will see to all your needs. Whilst here, pay a visit to Harry's Shack, which occupies a low bluff at the edge of the dunes. Its wide-framed seascapes make for a captivating setting in which to indulge in gut-busting burgers and mounds of fresh seafood. But if it's just a taste of seaside fun you're after, make for Morelli's, a fabled *gelato* parlour that has been doling out heavenly sundaes since 1927.

Seamus Heaney HomePlace

Seamus Heaney, by common consensus Ireland's greatest contemporary poet, was born in Bellaghy, an old plantation settlement near Lough Beg, in 1939. The closing lines of *Digging*, one of his first poems, captures his memories of his father digging potatoes and his grandfather digging turf as the poet puts pen to paper ("Between my finger and my thumb/The squat pen rests/I'll dig with it"). The marvellous Seamus Heaney HomePlace is a fitting tribute to the man and makes for an interesting day out. Reposed within the village's old police station, HomePlace is run through with Heaney's words and spirit, from the audios of the poet himself reading his poems to the trove of personal effects. Heaney is buried in the churchyard a few hundred metres from here, his grey headstone bearing the inscription 'Walk on air against your better judgement', a line from his poem *The Gravel Walks*.

(O) The poet's boyhood clothes; (L) Words from Heaney's poetry; (T) Imagery reflecting his works

THE Bogside Murals

Few places in Northern Ireland suffered as much during the Troubles as Derry, but to wander the streets today is to experience a city rejuvenated and, to an extent, reconciled, as symbolised by the Peace Bridge which snakes its way across the Foyle, linking the largely Unionist community on the east bank with the majority Nationalist community on the west bank. The most tangible reminder of the Troubles are *The Bogside Murals*, a series of large-scale paintings curated by a triumvirate of local artists in the 1990s. Whilst not affiliated to any political group, the murals remain divisive, a stark reminder of the violence that tore the city apart. But by the same token, they have become a major tourist attraction. Among the more striking images are those of a gas-mask-clad petrol bomber, and another entitled the *Death of Innocence*, which commemorates a 14-year-old girl, Annette McGavigan, caught in crossfire between the British Army and IRA. The murals have spawned further recent works of street art, such as *The Derry Girls*. For more insight into the Troubles, visit the Museum of Free Derry.

(L) The Dove of Peace mural; (T) Those riotous Derry Girls; (B) Murals evoke the pain of the Troubles

Derry City Walls

A circuit of Derry's walls is the essential introduction to the city. Built in the early seventeenth century and still remarkably complete, they enclose the compact historic core in a 1.6km loop of gates, bastions, ramparts and cannon. In places the walls rise as high as a two-storey house, wide enough on top to feel more like a street than a defensive structure. They also offer the clearest way to understand Derry's layered history. Within them are the old street pattern, St Columb's Cathedral and the Tower Museum. Beyond them lie the Bogside, the Fountain, the River Foyle and the modern city, which has been shaped by Plantation, siege, emigration, industry and of course, the Troubles. The views from the wals are not merely scenic. They are political, intimate and revealing, turning a stroll here into a walk through the arguments, scars and resilience of the "Maiden City".

(L) The Cathedral; (T) The Walls around Tower Museum; (B) Walking the wallls

Down & Armagh

Down and Armagh hold some of Northern Ireland's most attractive country, from lough shores and demesnes to mountains that dominate the southern skyline. Down is shaped by Strangford Lough, early Christian sites, seaside villages and the brooding Mournes, made for walking. Armagh's spiritual weight comes from St Patrick, who founded his first bishopric here, while its twin cathedrals, Georgian streets and the Ring of Gullion add layers of myth and ceremony.

Mount Stewart

Dramatically edging the western shore of Strangford Lough on the long and narrow Ards Peninsula stands Mount Stewart, the magnificent ancestral home of the Londonderry family. As entertaining as the guided tours of the house are – among the eccentric furnishings is a pair of hooves, now fashioned into inkwells, which belonged to Fighting Charlie, winner of the 1965 Ascot Gold Cup and ridden by the late, great Lester Piggott – it's the gardens that really enthral. Among the finest in all of Ireland, they were laid out in the 1920s by Edith, Marchioness of Londonderry, who was one serious horticulturalist, as well as a heavyweight society hostess and a pioneer pilot. Edith curated Italian and Spanish planting schemes, a funky shamrock garden complete with topiary harp, lake walks and lily woods, and a sea garden with date palms and rhododendrons to keep at bay the salt winds off the tidal lough. Craziest of all is the Dodo Terrace, flaunting various bits of giant statuary including the irritable-looking creatures themselves. Both Edith and her husband – the 7th Marquess of Londonderry – lie buried in an elaborate sarcophagi within the walled mausoleum, *Tír na nÓg,* high above the lake.

(L) The magnificent house

Mourne Mountains

The Mourne Mountains have long inspired writers, musicians and adventurers, from Percy French's songs to C S Lewis's *Chronicles of Narnia*. More recently, it has been *Game of Thrones*, much of which was filmed around these mountains – that has succeeded in establishing the Mournes as Northern Ireland's most valuable tourist draw. The Mournes are a relatively youthful set of granite mountains, with steep sides, moraines and occasional sheer cliffs, which gives them their sharp, jagged outline, but from a distance they appear much gentler. This is a truly ancient land, liberally sprinkled with prehistoric cairns and stone graves, many of which are said to mark the resting place of Irish chiefs. Yomp to the top of Slieve Donard (850m), Northern Ireland's highest peak and a steady five- to six-hour round trip. The heather-softened flanks of this magical mountain are not to be taken lightly, especially given the notoriously unpredictable local weather. But once at the summit, on a clear day you are rewarded with peerless views towards the Isle of Man and the coastlines of Wales and Scotland.

(L) Icy winter peaks; (T) Hikers setting out; (B) The beach at the nearby seaside town of Newcastle

Armagh City

Armagh barely registers on most people's itineraries, but this fine, big-hearted city simply begs to be explored. Begin with the city's twin ecclesiastical behemoths: the double-spired St Patrick's Church of Ireland Cathedral where, it is claimed, St Patrick founded his first church in 445AD – hence for many this is where the roots of Ireland lay – and, less than half a mile away on a neighbouring hill, St Patrick's Roman Catholic Cathedral, worth a lingering peek for its glittering wall-to-wall mosaics. Head down to The Mall, a vast and elegant oval green (it was once a racecourse) flanked by tree-lined promenades and rows of terraced Georgian houses. The city's real gem is the Armagh Robinson Library, which is not only the oldest library in all of Ireland but it also holds an extremely rare first edition of *Gulliver's Travels* annotated by Swift himself, as well as an early copy of Handel's *Messiah*; call ahead to visit. An easy local excursion is Navan Fort, home to the country's finest Iron Age legends and whose hill sites are exclusive to Ireland.

(O) The Mall; (L) Jonathan Swift's 'Gulliver's Travels' in Armagh Robinson Library; (T) Navan Fort; (B) St Patrick's Church of Ireland Cathedral

Ring of Gullion

(T) The vast volcanic landscape around the Ring of Gullion

An eerily volcanic landscape marking the border with County Louth in south Armagh, the Ring of Gullion has the honour of being the first ring dyke in the world to be geologically mapped; indeed, many experts claim it to be the finest ring dyke in the British Isles. The Ring occurred as a result of volcanic activity that convulsed this area around sixty million years ago, hence the 16km-wide circle of craggy mini-mountains you see today. Topping the lot is Slieve Gullion (573m), a mysteriously beautiful mountain rich in romantic legends, not least that concerning Cúchulainn (pronounced cooh-Cullen) – the hero of the Táin Bó Cúailnge (Cattle Raid of Cooley), who took his name here after slaying the hound (Cú) of the blacksmith Culainn. It's a short, sharp trek to the top, and worth it for the superlative and memorable outlook, both of the north and south of Ireland.

Tyrone & Fermanagh

Tyrone and Fermanagh form the inland west of Northern Ireland, rural, watery and quietly compelling. Tyrone stretches from Lough Neagh to the Sperrins, with emigration stories, stone circles and mountain trails giving depth to its farming landscape. Fermanagh is ruled by water, especially Lough Erne, where islands, castles, stately houses and caves make Enniskillen a natural base for slow exploration and unexpected discoveries across roads that reward patience and curiosity.

THE Sperrins

(T) A long route ahead

It is the largest mountain range in Northern Ireland, yet the Sperrins are in many ways forgotten – and that's just the way the locals like it. A succession of whaleback peaks, the highest of which is Sawel at 678m, the Sperrins get their name from the Irish *Na Speiríní*, meaning 'spurs of rock', though they are much smoother and more rounded than this implies. They date back 600 million years and comprise low-grade slate, and quartz, which is the source of the local tradition of panning for gold. Indeed, tales abound concerning the discovery of "gold in them thar hills", and you might still encounter the occasional panner testing the story's veracity. With vast tracks of hills, mile upon mile of bog and heather, and very little else for a long, long way, this is walking country par excellence: if you want to go the whole hog, the Central Sperrins Way is a fantastic 40km waymarked trail along the spine of the range, beginning at Gortin and ending in Moneyneany.

Ulster American Folk Park

Of all of Northern Ireland's American-heritage projects, the wonderful Ulster American Folk Park is by far the most rewarding. Set within some thirty acres of rolling countryside a few miles northwest of Omagh in County Tyrone, the park recalls how, during the eighteenth and nineteenth centuries, more than two million Ulster people left their homes to forge a new life across the Atlantic. Rich in originality, it's brought colourfully to life by an array of costumed characters going about their everyday lives among the shops and thatched cottages in the Old World and the log cabins and plantation houses of the New. Transporting you between the Old (Ulster) and the New (America) Worlds is a full-replica early 1800s ship, aboard which you'll 'experience' a tiny slither of the long and gruelling crossing across the North Atlantic. Try and coincide a visit with the rip-roaring Bluegrass Festival in early September, which invariably plays host to a stellar cast of musicians.

(O) The rustic buildings in the park; (L) The 'Old World';
(T) The Print Shop; (B) Performers at Bluegrass Festival

MasterCraft

Enniskillen

A cheerful little market town framed by two narrow ribbons of water connecting the Lower and Upper sections of Lough Erne, Enniskillen happily lays claim to being Northern Ireland's only island town. Contained within its delightful streetscape, a few must-sees include Headhunters, a barber's shop-cum-railway museum (yes, really); the Buttermarket, a nineteenth-century stone dairy market now home to resident craftsfolk; and the enduringly popular Blakes of the Hollow, once described by the Irish writer Colm Tóibín as 'a cathedral of a pub'. Go see for yourself. From Enniskillen it's a short way to Lough Erne, two connected lakes that epitomise Fermanagh's profoundly important relationship with water: indeed, an old adage maintains that for six months Lough Erne is in Fermanagh, and for the rest of the year Fermanagh is in Lough Erne. It's all very much *Swallows and Amazons* territory: boats, fishing, uninhabited islands and monastic ruins, ripe for endless exploration, whatever your age.

(L) Enniskillen Castle; (T) Lough Erne; (B) The Blakes bar

Finn Lough

Bubble domes to sleep under the stars, split-level lake houses with the dreamiest views, and a restaurant with a tasting menu that is out of this world, Finn Lough delivers with finesse. Nestled quietly on a sheltered stretch of Lough Erne, with views of Boa Island across the water, this innovative getaway sits on a little peninsula in Enniskillen, Fermanagh. An adults-only oasis, this is the place to come for superb service, a serene lakeside setting and restorative spa treatments. Follow the Elements spa nature trail along the edge of the lake to luxuriate in the heated saltwater floatation pool followed by the Finnish sauna, before a cooling plunge in the lake; then onto the aromatherapy sauna, hot tub and relaxation room. Emerge renewed in mind, body and soul. Cycle or walk the woodland paths, watch a film in the cinema, luxuriate in the breakfast hamper delivered to your door, grab a lazy lunch in the bar and be blown away by fine dining.

(O) The sauna with its lake views; (L) The bubble domes are perfect for stargazing; (T) One of the lovely lake houses

Marble Arch Caves

There is something inherently fascinating about the subterranean world, and so it is with the Marble Arch Caves, which were first discovered in 1895 by Frenchman Edouard Martel and Dublin zoologist Henry Lyster Jameson, although they weren't revealed to the public until 1985. Following a pleasant little walk down through the reserve, the guided tour begins with a short boat journey along the underground Cladagh River, before continuing on terra firma through a succession of lofty chambers and tightly wound passages. Throughout, clusters of weirdly shaped stalactites and stalagmites, as well as other impressive formations such as flowstones and scallops (sculpted indentations caused by water flow) constantly vie for your attention. As is standard practice in the world of show caves, many of these formations have been assigned peculiar names, like Porridge Pot and Guardian Angel, although it does occasionally require a degree of lateral thinking to understand why.

(L) Inside the atmospheric caves; (T) A guided tour explains all the different formations; (B) On the boat tour

Stairway TO Heaven

A wonderful hike seemingly into the heavens, this walk demands a certain level of fitness in order to ascend the steep incline, but the arrival at the top is reward enough. Covering the biggest expanse of blanket bog in Ireland, the Stairway to Heaven walk, also known as the Cuilcagh Boardwalk Trail, takes you over gravel tracks, boardwalk and, you guessed it, steps. The route is just under 15km-long and is rated as difficult, mainly due to the gradual incline and the 1.5km-long steep staircase. Expect it to take around four hours to complete. It's located in the UNESCO Marble Arch Geopark, a special conservation area. Along the route, enjoy views of the protected bogland around you and the natural flora and fauna endemic to the area. At the top, stop for a breather and soak in the views before a more leisurely return back down to earth.

(L) The ascent

Publishing information

Ireland • 100 Legendary Places
Editor: Sarah Clark
Designer: Michał Ptasznik
Picture Manager: Tom Smyth
Production Operations Manager: Katie Bennett
Publishing Technology Manager: Rebeka Davies
Head of Publishing: Sarah Clark

Our selection
Ireland • 100 Legendary Places offers our curation of the most exceptional destinations in the country, with content drawn from *Rough Guides Ireland* and *100 Best Places in Ireland*, originally edited by Kate Drynan. Contributors to these books included: Siobhan Canavan, Kate Drynan, Alannah Hopkin, George Keenan, Norm Longley, Niall O'Donaghue and Mundy Walsh.

First Edition 2026

ISBN: 9781835296486

Printed by Finidr in Czech Republic

MIX
Paper | Supporting responsible forestry
FSC® C014138

A catalogue record for this book is available from the British Library.

Distribution
UK, Ireland and Europe
Apa Publications (UK) Ltd; mail@roughguides.com
United States and Canada
Two Rivers; ips@ ingramcontent.com
Australia and New Zealand
Woodslane; info@woodslane.com.au
Worldwide
Apa Publications (UK) Ltd; mail@roughguides.com

Special Sales, Content Licensing and CoPublishing
Rough Guides can be purchased in bulk quantities at discounted prices. We can create special editions, personalized jackets and corporate imprints tailored to your needs.
mail@roughguides.com; http://roughguides.com

EU Representative
LOGOS EUROPE, 9 rue Nicolas Poussin, 17000, LA ROCHELLE, France
Contact@logoseurope.eu; +33 (0) 667937378

Caption key
(L) = left
(R) = right
(T) = top
(B) = bottom
(O) = opposite

Photo credits

Adrian Langtry/Shutterstock 55T
AirSwing Media 129T
Alamy 28/29, 36, 37B, 37T, 44/45, 48/49, 70/71, 76/77, 90/91, 132/133, 135R, 164/165, 192/193, 204/205
Allen Kiely/ Tourism Ireland 74
Arigna Mining Experience LTD 168
Arno-nl 172/173
Arthur Ward/Tourism Ireland 200
Belfast Political Tour 195T
Bernie Brown/Tourism Ireland 203BL, 203BR
Big Smoke Studio 142, 144/145
Brian Morrison/ Tourism Ireland 72
Castle Leslie Estate 46, 47B
Celtic Routes 27T
Chaosheng Zhang 143BL, 143BR, 143TR
Chris Hill/Tourism Ireland 7BR, 20, 61B, 61T, 95B, 103B, 109T, 109B, 113B, 131BL, 146, 185BR, 190, 191TR, 198/199, 219B, 235B
Christian McLeod Photography/Tourism Ireland 2/3, 150, 157T
Christopher Heaney/Tourism Ireland 201T
Clare County Council 7MR, 130, 131TR
Colin Shanahan/DigiCol Photography 86, 87B, 87T
Conor McCabe Photography 56
Courtesy Brian Morrison 7BL, 34/35
Courtesy Irish National Stud and Gardens 30, 31B, 31T
Courtesy Marcelline Roulleau 13B, 13T
Courtesy Milestone Inventive 147T
Courtesy shane@howthadventures.com 19B, 19T
David Sexton/Tourism Northern Ireland 229TR
Derry City and Strabane District Council 210, 211T
Diana Jarvis/Tourism Ireland 228
Dillon Osborne/Tourism Ireland 211B
Dylan Vaughan Photography 75BR
Enda Cavanagh for Diageo 8
Finn Lough 232, 233L, 233R
Fáilte Ireland 22/23, 32, 33R, 55B, 57BL, 57BR, 58/59, 60, 63L, 66/67, 69BR, 69TR, 80, 83BL, 83BR, 99T, 122/123, 157B, 166, 167L, 169B, 169T, 170, 171BR, 171TR
Fáilte Ireland/Tourism Ireland 40, 43R, 47T, 50, 51BL, 51BR, 51TR, 75BL, 88, 92, 93BL, 93BR, 93TR, 98, 176
Gardiner Mitrchel/Tourism Northern Ireland 224, 231T
Gareth McCormack/Fáilte Ireland/Tourism Ireland 136, 148, 149T, 149B, 158/159, 163BL, 167R, 181L
Gareth Wray Photography 182, 184, 185BL, 185TR, 212/213
George Munday/Tourism Ireland 78
Government of Ireland National Monuments Service Photographic Unit 52
Harbour Productions/Christopher Heaney 191BL
Hu O'Reilly 100
Joshua Hannah/Tourism Ireland 230
Kevin Cummins/Apa Publications 194
Liana Modonova 7TL
LMK PHOTOGRAPHY 208
Longford Tourism 63R
Lukasz Warzecha/Fáilte Ireland 163BR
Navan Centre and Fort 221TR
Niamh Whitty/Fáilte Ireland 156
Noel Carrigy 62
Paul Lindsay/Tourism Ireland 234, 235T
Press Eye/Darren Kidd 229BR
Rathcrogan Visitor Center 171BL
Resolute Photography/Failte Ireland 103T
Rob Durston/Tourism Ireland 231B
Shannon Group plc 125T, 125B
Sheikh Haaris 120
Shutterstock 10/11, 14/15, 16, 17L, 17R, 24, 25BL, 33L, 39BL, 39BR, 43L, 64, 81B, 82, 84/85, 106/107, 108. 110, 111L, 111R, 116, 117T, 117B, 118, 119L, 119R, 131BR, 134, 135L, 138/139, 141T, 141B, 152/153, 163TR, 183T, 186/187, 191BR, 195B, 209B, 209T, 214, 218, 229BL, 236/237
Sligo Tourism 160, 162
Spike Island Management 104/105
SuperStock 25BR, 96/97, 124, 126/127, 140
Tipperary Tourism 95T
Tourism Ireland 7TR, 12, 18, 25TR, 26, 27B, 38, 39TR, 42, 75TR, 79L, 79R, 81T, 83TR, 94, 99B, 102, 112, 113T, 114/115, 128, 129B, 147B, 154, 155BR, 155TR, 155BL, 174, 175T, 175B, 178/179, 180, 181R, 183B, 197L, 202, 203TR, 206, 207L, 207R, 216/217, 220, 221BL, 221BR, 222/223, 226/227
Tourism Northern Ireland 188, 196, 197R, 201B, 219T
Tristan Hutchinson Photography 54, 57TR, 65T, 65B, 68, 69BL

Cover credit: The Cliffs of Moher in County Clare **iStock**

Ireland IS waiting

Make the **legend** your own